"We get formed from the outside in, but we lead from the inside out. T. J. Addington explains this process with clarity and conviction. In an age of superficiality, he will guide you to the deeper places of influence and change."

JOHN C. ORTBERG
Author, speaker, and senior pastor of Menlo Park Presbyterian Church in Menlo Park, CA

"I've been a fan of T. J. Addington for a long time. I'm a wiser and better leader because of his writings. But *Deep Influence* is his most important contribution yet. Every young leader will gain decades of leadership wisdom forged in the painful trenches of reality. Veteran leaders will be inspired to finish strong."

GENE APPEL
Senior pastor of Eastside Christian Church in Anaheim, CA

"Any leader willing to offer his story authentically and invite others to do the same is an author worth paying attention to. T. J. is a man who has cultivated his inner life around the person of Christ and allowed God to shape and reshape his heart, mind, relationships, and priorities. He has led from a spiritual depth and now is sharing his biblical and transformational insights in *Deep Influence*. I'm delighted to encourage Christian leaders to consider each chapter herein with prayerful seriousness and godly attentiveness."

STEPHEN A. MACCHIA
Founder and president of Leadership Transformations, director of the Pierce Center at Gordon-Conwell Seminary, and author of *Becoming A Healthy Church* and *Crafting A Rule of Life*

"My friend T. J. Addington is a wise leadership guru, and *Deep Influence* is his most profound book on the subject! A seasoned, reflective practitioner, T. J. masterfully tackles the most challenging terrain of leadership—the inner life of the leader— along with the empowering practices each leader must cultivate. Few books effectively deal with leadership from the inside out. This is one of the best!"

EDMUND CHAN
Leadership mentor at Covenant EFC and founder of
Global Alliance of Intentional Disciplemaking Churches

"As a wife, mother, and educator, I've been challenged and reminded through this book of what it truly means to live an authentic life in Christ. It begins with humility and honesty— seeking the heart of God and living out all that He calls us to be. It is through this personal relationship with Christ that we are then able to be molded and crafted to become effective in our leadership roles and to influence others. If your desire is to live out your calling with great effectiveness as you reflect Christ to a seeking world, *Deep Influence* is just the navigation you need!"

MELISSA LARSON
Adjunct professor of Biblical and Theological Studies at
University of Northwestern

"If you are not yet convinced that the most difficult challenge you will face as a leader is in 'self-leadership,' then read *Deep Influence*. My dear friend T. J. Addington sharpened his ministry leadership out of the depths of life experience even as God granted and grew him into a major leadership role for the global church. Deepened by a vital spiritual relationship with God, he enriches fellow leaders with practical wisdom toward deep influence for God's purposes."

RAMESH RICHARD, ThD, PhD
President of RREACH, professor at Dallas Seminary, and founder of Trainers of Pastors International Coalition (TOPIC)

"*Deep Influence* is an invitation to listen to a seasoned leader's voice dripping with the life-giving wisdom of Jesus. The practices in this book will lead to an exegesis of the heart and guide the reader into the lifelong journey of allowing God to mold 'who we are,' which informs 'what we do.'"

TOM SMITH
Pastor, husband, cofounder of Rhythm of Life, and author of *Raw Spirituality: The Rhythms of the Jesus Life*

"*Deep Influence* cuts to the core of leadership and returns character to the central place it occupies in God's eyes. I have shelves full of books on leadership, but this one leaves you knowing you can be better and lead better. It is significant without being tedious, direct but not discouraging. Buy it, read it, mark it up, and read it again. Addington ought to be on top of the pile."

DAVID W. HEGG, DMin
Pastor, adjunct professor, and author of *The Obedience Option*

"*Deep Influence*, every chapter, was a deep dive into my motives, methods, mind, mission calling, leadership style, and relationships that brought me to a place of unexpected and unconventional light, revealing a clear, fresh, exciting perspective to press forward. T. J. humbly said it well—'Depth matters'—as he carefully and biblically aimed at my life through the person of Jesus Christ and hit my inner target: the sanctum of my heart. This book is a transparent, transformational leadership mirror that leads to intentional joy and freedom. Ephesians 2:10 came alive in me, and it will in you."

DOUG FAGERSTROM, DMin
Senior vice president of Converge and author of *The Ministry Staff Member* and *The Volunteer*

"With skill and clarity, T. J. Addington argues that leadership is not about technique—it is about character. What matters most is not *how* we lead but from what *source* we choose to lead. Whether you are a ministry leader or a leader in the marketplace, this book describes the practices that will enable you to lead from the inside out. If you want to grow as a leader, this book is a great place to start."

GEORGE DAVIS, PhD
Senior pastor of Hershey Free Church in Hershey, PA

"*Deep Influence* draws an effective map for exploring the inner life so often neglected by today's image-conscious leader. T. J.'s emphasis on personal integrity, authenticity, and emotional intelligence offers a healthy antidote to the toxic influence of every leader's shadow side. His practical, personal counsel encourages, challenges, and inspires every leader to pursue the slower, more intentional, inside-out path to deeper, lasting impact in ministry."

RUSS KINKADE, PsyD
Psychologist and executive VP of Shepherds Ministries

T. J. ADDINGTON

DEEP
INFLUENCE

UNSEEN PRACTICES THAT WILL REVOLUTIONIZE YOUR LEADERSHIP

NavPress

A NAVPRESS RESOURCE PUBLISHED IN ALLIANCE WITH TYNDALE HOUSE PUBLISHERS, INC.

NavPress is the publishing ministry of The Navigators, an international Christian organization and leader in personal spiritual development. NavPress is committed to helping people grow spiritually and enjoy lives of meaning and hope through personal and group resources that are biblically rooted, culturally relevant, and highly practical.

For more information, visit www.NavPress.com.

Library of Congress Cataloging-in-Publication Data

Addington, T. J.

    Deep influence : unseen practices that will revolutionize your leadership / T. J. Addington.

      pages cm

    ISBN 978-1-61291-807-5

1. Leadership--Religious aspects—Christianity.   2. christian leadership.   I. Title.

    BV4597.53.L43A335 2015

    253—dc23   2014034216

ISBN 978-1-61291-807-5

Printed in the United States of America

21	20	19	18	17	16	15
8	7	6	5	4	3	2

To my father,

engineer, theologian, church planter, evangelist,

physician, surgeon, author, teacher, and mentor to many.

Most importantly a man of deep influence

who met his Lord on November 19, 2012.

To the Directional Team of

the EFCA and ReachGlobal,

people of deep influence,

with whom it is a joy to work.

Contents

Acknowledgments

All books are cooperative efforts. I am grateful to Mary
Ann, my wife, for her encouragement in this journey and
her willingness to let me spend the hours necessary to write.
Our friends, Grant and Carol, graciously provided us a place
to write each summer while enjoying the Gallatin Valley
in Montana.

My colleagues in ReachGlobal were the first group to
hear these concepts and provided valuable feedback and
encouragement along the way. I am deeply indebted to my
publisher, Don Pape, who believed in this book and became
its cheerleader; and to my editor, Brian Smith, whose edit-
ing skills made the book better. I also thank the many staff

members of NavPress and Tyndale, whose expertise brought the publication of this project to fruition.

Finally, this book would not have been written without people of deep influence who impacted my life and modeled what it means to influence another. In particular I owe a great debt of gratitude to Dr. Walter C. Kaiser Jr., for whom I served as teaching assistant for four years at Trinity Evangelical Divinity School (1979–1983) and who left an indelible imprint on my life and leadership. To the many more whose imprint I also bear, I say thank you!

CHAPTER ONE

FORGED ON THE INSIDE

Character, courage, wisdom, integrity, humility, spiritual depth, endurance, perseverance, kindness, and vision. What do all of these qualities have in common? They all come from a place deep inside our hearts—the hidden recesses of our souls, whose channels lead to deep veins of God's work and molding. That which is most *central* to what we are and who we become cannot be directly seen by others, but its impact is felt by those we lead, and it determines the depth of our leadership, our character, our vision, and the philosophy from which we lead.

That's why I call these qualities, collectively, *deep influence*. Too much attention is paid to leadership techniques and far too little to the kind of heart and mind from which the best leadership emanates. All the right techniques cannot make up for an absence of a deep inner core, molded and richly forged over time by Christ: the source of the best leadership because it reflects His mind and heart.

This book is about the *inner life* of a leader, the practices he or she cultivates, which leads ultimately to the most profound leadership of all—deep influence. There are many leadership styles, but in the end the leaders who have the deepest influence on their organizations and the people around them share a common theme: They have cultivated their inner lives around the person of Christ and allowed Him to handcraft and transform their hearts, minds, relationships, and priorities.

This inner transformation changes the leadership equation in numerous ways: It changes our understanding of Christ's grace (our hearts); it enhances our learning to think like Christ (our minds); it guides us to treat people as Christ would (our relationships); and it focuses our lives around those things that are most important to Him (our priorities). In other words, it touches all of what makes us, *us*! Such a spiritual metamorphosis allows us to lead out of spiritual, relational, and emotional health, as well as a reservoir stocked with *Him*, spilling out in our words, actions, and intentions.

Leadership opportunities have come to me since I was a teenager. What I did not realize then—or even in my twenties and thirties—was that the transformation that leads to depth takes time. Nor did I imagine the cost of the leadership journey. While I would not want to do anything else, who I am today is the result of God's gracious and sometimes painful molding over several decades of leading in a variety of settings. Today my leadership is better—only partly because of better technique, but mostly because of what God has done in my interior life, which informs and influences all that I am.

My first significant leadership position as a pastor of a new church plant ended, from a human perspective, in a spectacular failure. I resigned—dreams shattered, clinically depressed—and then watched the church split after I left. What I did not know then was how God would use that event and its pain to make me who I am today. It was forging on the inside that I needed; God did an inner work that has directed the rest of my life.

His work in me over these years is like a vein of gold, of which miners dream as they work the bowels of the mountain. It is wealth attained with much hard work and at significant cost. But when the vein is struck, we know it was worth the effort.

At fifty-seven I have many battle scars from the leadership arena. My skin is thicker, heart softer, actions more measured, and wisdom deeper. The gains have been hard-won and worth each lesson learned and each facet of character etched. I enjoy deeper influence today because of the Spirit's work in the interior recesses of my life.

The best leaders—those who make the greatest impact

over the longest period of time, who lead with the greatest wisdom and discernment for long-term results and the building of the best teams—lead from a spiritual depth. The more developed one's spiritual core, the greater one's influence to impact our world in significant ways for a cause greater than ourselves.

I am not minimizing the skill necessary to lead. Leadership clearly requires gifting. My conviction, however, is that the *best* leadership does not simply come as a result of cultivating skill alone but is significantly influenced by the men or women we have allowed God to mold us into. The best leaders are characterized by passionately held values, thoughtful reflection, and authentic humility. Many people have leadership skills, but fewer people have the *foundation* of truly deep influence.

The writer of Proverbs reminds us, "Above all else, guard your heart, for everything you do flows from it" (Proverbs 4:23). Jesus told His followers that our words, actions, and thoughts all come from the reservoir of our hearts (see Matthew 15:18-20). What has filled that reservoir spills over in our leadership. Fill it with Him and He will spill out.

The preponderance of books on leadership focus on what good leaders *do*, how they *act*, or the strategies they *implement*. Some of these books provide real insight into good leadership principles. But these are not the most *important* issues in leadership, nor are they where leadership *starts*. Great leadership starts deep inside, and the best leaders belong in a category set apart. Their uniqueness lies not first in their ability, but in a set of intentional practices that they nurture. Those practices, combined with leadership ability, make the difference between the average leader and a leader of deep influence.

Much of what passes for leadership is simply a position of authority, but true leadership is not about authority. Those who declare "I am the leader and this is what we are going to do" are rarely true leaders; some situations require this approach, but they're the exceptions. These are the words of people in authority who *think* that leadership is constituted by their telling others what they should do. They are not only wrong, but they do not understand that *influence* is far more powerful than *authority*.

Others think that if they adopt the latest leadership theory or the style of leaders they admire, they too will lead well. This flavor-of-the-month leadership leads to cynicism among staff as the leadership techniques and philosophy change with the winds.

Many believe that the core of great leadership is action; they are constantly on the move, looking for the next strategy or initiative to pursue. It's true, leaders *are* people of action, but not thoughtlessly or frantically so. The most effective action comes out of deep thinking, spiritual insight, personal understanding, a defining internal compass, and the ability to connect the dots of opportunity, needs, organizational ability, and strategy. The question is not whether leaders are people of action but whether their action comes from a depth of inner conviction, rather than from an addiction to motion.

WHO A LEADER IS COMES
BEFORE WHAT A LEADER DOES

Great leadership starts with *who* we are and then extends to *what* we do. It stems from a rich combination of personal health, spiritual transformation, and intentional practices that allow us to influence others toward the fulfillment of a mission.

Think of those who have motivated you toward great things, who have brought out the very best in you. Was it their leadership skills or was it something about their character and vision that touched your life? Probably you saw in them authenticity, conviction, integrity, wisdom, vision, and spiritual depth, as well as ability. We have an instinctive desire to collaborate with people who possess these qualities. Our desire to follow is stirred by the deep influence of a transformed leader.

These qualities *cannot* be microwaved instantly into a person but are forged over time by a set of practices that eventually separate deep leaders from shallow leaders. The difference may not be visible when a leader is young and leading out of energy and fresh vision. It does become clear in later years when a depth of maturity is either evident or absent.

In my fifties, I believe that age has much to do with leadership depth. I thought I was a pretty good leader when I was young, and I believe that young leaders can be good leaders. But because spiritual depth and ability are developed and honed over time—and have so much to do with our leadership effectiveness—I believe that great leadership is usually revealed in middle age and after. Those who lead well in early years and are intentional in developing personal depth can become great leaders in their latter years. Many who seem to lead well in early years don't end their leadership careers well. Often they've had innate leadership ability but haven't done the necessary work to nurture the qualities that would eventually make them leaders of deep influence.

If you are a leader in your twenties or thirties, let me say from experience: When we are young we are never as good as we think we are. But if we nurture the practices of highly influential leaders along the way, in later years we may become better leaders than we think we are. Most leadership implosions can be traced back to the *neglect* of certain practices. Those who lead well over the long haul and become leaders of deep influence can trace their success to the intentional nurture of those same practices.

If there is one thing you gain from considering these hidden practices with me, I hope it is that the core disciplines of leadership relate less to *what we do* (important as that is) and more to *who we are*, which informs what we do. If we keep these priorities in order, it will revolutionize our influence over time.

DEPTH MATTERS

One of my greatest fears is that I would settle for a shallow heart, becoming distracted by strategies, activities, and "accomplishing the mission"—all good pursuits, but not the foundation of lasting influence. Growing deep with God and allowing His character to transform me ensures that my leadership emanates from a mature spiritual and emotional core. Shallow hearts and minds do not lead to deep influence!

King Saul in the Old Testament is an example of a leader who started well but neglected the practices of an influential leader, resulting in a terrible finish. In his early years he looked and acted like a leader. He was described as "an impressive young man. There was no one more impressive among the Israelites than he. He stood a head taller than anyone else" (1 Samuel 9:2, HCSB). In the early years of his reign he pulled off some impressive victories, but there were signs that all was not well.

Saul believed that his leadership was about him, rather than about a stewardship given him by God to manage on God's behalf. He ignored the prophet Samuel's instructions, and over time his leadership deteriorated and his heart revealed its true shallowness, until he lost first the blessing of God, and then his life on the battlefield.

While Saul started well, it was the lack of depth in his spiritual life—of wisdom and a moral compass in decision making, and of a transformed inner core—that resulted in his long-term decline. As a result he made poor decisions, listened to bad advisors, displayed low emotional intelligence, and undermined his own leadership. Saul operated from a *shallow* heart.

In an interesting comparison between the description of Saul as "an impressive young man," the prophet Samuel was instructed by God to go to Bethlehem to anoint one of the sons of Jesse as king in Saul's place (see 1 Samuel 16). He arrived and immediately assumed that Eliab, apparently the oldest or the most imposing, must be the one; he looked like kingly material. "But the LORD said to Samuel, 'Do not consider his appearance or his height, for I have rejected him. The LORD does not look at the things people look at. People look at the outward appearance, but the LORD looks at the heart'" (1 Samuel 16:7). Instead of Eliab and the others, God had chosen the youngest, David, who was out tending sheep at the time, indicating his humble position.

God has an intriguing way of choosing leaders that seems counterintuitive from the world's vantage point. Consider Deborah in the time of the judges; Paul, a former persecutor of the church; the disciples, many of whom we would not choose to change the world; Joseph, a former convict; Moses, a has-been who came into leadership after leading sheep for forty years; and the list could go on.

What God is looking for is the depth of heart, faith, and wisdom that comes from inner maturity. The difference between Saul and David was the difference between a shallow heart and a deep heart. David's depth was evident at an early age—he was about sixteen years old or so when he took on Goliath—and deepened during the years between his anointing as king and the death of Saul, when he became the leader of Judah and then of Israel.

The books of 1 and 2 Samuel are instructive for those who want to lead well. Clearly David was a gifted leader. He engendered great loyalty from those he led; he was strategic in his leadership, was undaunted by adversity, and proved tenacious in achieving his goals. We know, however, from the Psalms that he also possessed an inner depth that came from his relationship and dependence on God. One wonders where David found the time to go this deep spiritually when he was also the CEO of Israel, but clearly he did. And the long-term effectiveness of David as compared to Saul is the proof that this matters.

A LEADERSHIP PERSPECTIVE OF TIME

Depth takes time. It cannot be hurried!

Many leaders mistake short-term success for long-term effectiveness. They are so concerned about their success in the moment and in proving their leadership ability that they don't think long-term toward becoming leaders of deep influence. This is often true of highly gifted ministry leaders who are so driven to prove they can succeed that they do not take the time to develop a deep core. They settle for surface wins.

Young leaders need to understand that God wants to bless your leadership. But more than immediate results, He wants you to press into Him and into those practices that will make your leadership successful and deep over the long run. Being persistently intentional about those practices rather than in a hurry for success makes the difference between those who settle for shallow leadership and those who develop deep influence.

Where did the depth of Moses' leadership come from? As a young leader he was impetuous and careless and ended up having to flee Egypt, even though he had been raised in the royal household. God gave Moses *forty years* to develop his leadership heart and soul before He drafted him for *the* decisive moment in Old Testament redemption history! Moses looked like a leadership failure early on. Many of us do as well. But not to God. God used that failure to build into Moses a dependence on Him rather than on Moses' own wisdom. It took time, but an impatient and shallow leader became one of the greatest, deepest, wisest leaders in the history of God's people.

Where did David's depth come from? It came from his time as a young shepherd out with the sheep; there he developed his relationship with God. It also came through the pain of becoming the object of Saul's wrath, even after being anointed king by Samuel and serving Saul well. David had to live like a pariah, constantly on the run, relying on the only help he had—God. I am sure there were many moments in those years on the run when David felt like a failure. But his depth was forged in both joy and pain, and in choosing to press into God.

Or consider Joseph, who was sold into slavery at seventeen and spent ten years in God's waiting room (mostly in prison) before he emerged ready for God's leadership assignment at age twenty-seven. And not because he didn't love and trust God! God used the prison years to build into Joseph's leadership exactly what would be needed for his next assignment—depth that could not be forged in any other way than through hard times.

God is never in a hurry with His plans for our lives. *We*

are often in a hurry, but *He* never is. In fact, it does not bother God to take eighty years to prepare someone for His mission (Moses), or years languishing in a jail (Joseph), or time spent on the wrong side of truth (Paul). God never feels rushed as He builds in us those qualities that make for a person of deep influence. What He desires from us is not hurriedness but humble, patient cooperation as He develops the very traits that will make us who He wants us to be for His purposes.

Wisdom, character, spiritual depth, perspective, and the lessons that come from deep wounds all take time to develop. It is possible to be theologically precise at a young age, but it is with the passage of years that we grow and add depth to our understanding.

As a young pastor I was well trained to exegete the biblical text and communicate God's truth, but I was shallow in real-life experience. My preaching and teaching is far better today, not because I have learned to exegete the text better but because my experience helps me to better exegete life and people. No amount of intelligence can make up for the schooling that comes only from negotiating the vagaries of life. Depth takes time.

In my younger days I was too easily discouraged in the face of opposition—and I had my share of opposition. The passage of time has taught me that I don't need to be anxious about many of the circumstances I face because God acts in His time. That lesson could only be learned in the fire of hardship and discouragement. Time, experience, perseverance, and God's work in my life have given me a resolve that I did not have in earlier days.

God is more concerned about the depth of our leadership than about the outward success of our leadership. If we are intentional in our cooperation with His plan, He will build that depth into our lives. I've already mentioned the "great failure" that I faced early in my leadership career. God saw it differently. He used that episode to humble me, to teach me to rely on Him and to press into His grace; and that early "failure" has informed whatever success I have attained since. Depth comes more often from failure and pain than from success! It is in the tough times that we are invited, like Moses and David, to go deep with God. What looks like failure to us is often part of God's plan to develop us as leaders. It is a wonderful thing to come to the place where we have nothing to rely on but Him.

ABOUT ME OR HIM?

A fundamental difference between Saul's and David's leadership was its focus. For Saul, leadership was about himself. *He* was king, *he* had the power, and he believed that *he* could make decisions without heeding godly advice. Or even God's advice. Essentially his leadership was self-centered and selfish.

Leaders who believe that everything is about them (and there are many) become arrogant, believing their own press and concluding that since they got into the position it must mean that they are pretty good and have adequate wisdom to make the right decisions. Christian leaders are not immune to this temptation. While we all claim (and perhaps believe) that we are serving Christ in our leadership, our pursuit of success is often at least as much about us as it is about the One we serve.

Many leaders in the Christian arena are indistinguishable from leaders in the secular arena, except that they impose a *spiritual vocabulary* on their leadership plans. The question of whether our leadership is truly centered around us or around God is one that requires careful reflection and heart analysis. We must question the motives of leaders who are so driven that they hurt people in their paths, intent on having their own way to reach their own dreams. Where there is arrogance in leadership—Christian or secular—leadership is more about the leader than the mission or the One behind the mission.

Every leader is building something; it is the nature of leadership. *For* whom we are building is the trickier question. Whether in business or in ministry, leaders who have not gone deep with God in inner transformation can only be building something for themselves: It is the default position of our lower, untransformed nature. We are fooling ourselves if we build on anything other than a significantly transformed inner life that has been so influenced with the priorities of Christ that they become our priorities.

God-centered leaders operate by a different set of practices that come from inner transformation. For them, leadership is a trust. Peter made this clear when he said to the elders of the church,

Be shepherds of God's flock that is under your care,
watching over them—not because you must, but
because you are willing, as God wants you to be; not
pursuing dishonest gain, but eager to serve; not lording
it over those entrusted to you, but being examples to the
flock. And when the Chief Shepherd appears, you will
receive the crown of glory that will never fade away.
1 PETER 5:2-4

What is intriguing in this passage is that Peter eliminates the motives that drive many leaders—money, power, and personal agendas. He makes it clear that our leadership is simply a trust given to us by the true leader of the church—Christ—and that the core of our leadership comes from who we are and the depth that has been developed within. It's from such character that a man or woman of God is to lead, by being an example to the flock. The most powerful influence we have as leaders comes from our conduct, which is the outward expression of our inner core.

Our life examples are even more important than our leadership ability because our lives are the authentication of our character, giving credence to our leadership. All of us have met leaders whose personal examples did not cause us to want to follow.

An example worth following is often the missing element in those who give leadership to the church. They may have leadership skills, but their lives do not reflect a deep inner core of spiritual maturity, wisdom, understanding, and attitudes that come from a transformed heart. Too often theirs is a shallow leadership that is more about their agenda for the congregation than God's agenda. Theirs is a leadership that has not been steeped in God. (For an extended discussion of what God looks for in church leadership, see my previous book, *High Impact Church Boards*.)

God has an agenda for how our ministries contribute to His work. Our awareness of that agenda and the ways we can serve His plan comes out of a relationship with God, out of dependence on Him, out of an understanding of what God wants to do in our world. This is not primarily about our wisdom but about His presence; our understanding of Him informs all that we do as leaders under His lordship.

The more our leadership is informed by God, by His agenda, and by His character within us, the deeper our influence. Our influence is actually His influence lived through us!

We become His agents of influence when our lives are deeply connected to and informed by Him. Our leadership is an extension of His leadership, which is precisely why Peter calls elders in the church "shepherds" who work *for* the "Chief Shepherd" (1 Peter 5:2-4). *Any eternal influence we exercise is an extension of His influence.*

The greatest compliment anyone can pay us is that the example of our lives influenced him or her to go deeper with Jesus. That is influence of the deepest kind. It is Christ lived through us.

INSIDE OUT

We live in a time when the demands on leaders are weighty and complex. None of us has extra time to spare. Our calendars are so packed that we hardly have time to breathe, and we end up living on fumes.

This creates a dilemma for anyone who desires to become a leader of deep influence because that desire demands the one thing we have so little of—time. I have said that leaders of deep influence are fundamentally different from other leaders. They live differently, they prioritize differently, they think differently, and they use their time differently.

They understand that depth must be nurtured. They have the same amount of time as other leaders, but they *use* that time differently and more intentionally. They think long-term rather than short-term and are determined to go the distance, rather than win the sprint.

The typical out-of-control schedules that characterize many leaders' lives are not congruent with becoming leaders of deep influence. Nor are these kinds of schedules necessary. Often they reflect more a lack of wisdom and intentionality than successful leadership. A packed calendar page looks impressive, but it is often the prelude to personal trouble when lack of depth becomes a liability that not even the most frenetic energy can cover.

The question for us is not whether we will work hard or endure seasons of intense time commitment. The question is how we will allocate our time and priorities for long-term leadership success, over against short-term leadership wins.

Will we make space in our busy schedules for God—so that He can inform our hearts and mold our character, so that we hear His voice?

Leaders of deep influence have developed habits that allow them to become what they are. For example,

- They are more reflective.
- They take the time to think more deeply.
- They spend more time understanding themselves and those they lead.
- They are more deeply committed to understanding God and His Word and discerning His direction.
- They ask more and better questions.
- They take more time to evaluate success and effectiveness in their own lives and in the ministries they lead.
- They do less so that they can accomplish more.
- They think long-term rather than short-term.
- They are more concerned about the quality of their inner lives than the success of their outer lives.
- They are deeply sensitive to the voice of God in their own lives and leadership.

The common denominator is that leaders of deep influence use their time differently in order to grow leadership from the *inside out*—leadership that reveals itself as wise, strategic, Christ-centered. Instead of focusing on the end product, they first focus on the source of their leadership.

They develop an inner reservoir of spiritual, personal, and emotional health that results in healthy leadership.

DEEP INFLUENCERS BEFORE US

Each of us owes a debt of gratitude to those who have exercised deep influence on our lives. They helped shape who we are today. They paid the price to become people of deep influence, and their investments have paid off in our leadership.

It was 1970 when Rev. John Stott came to do a "mission" at the local Anglican church in Hong Kong. I had moved to Hong Kong in 1960 with my parents, who were missionaries with the EFCA (Evangelical Free Church of America).

At age fourteen, I was transfixed by Dr. Stott's clear, exegetical, humble presentations of the gospel over the course of a week. I drank in his teaching and analyzed how he handled the text. But more significant were the personal conversations Dr. Stott had with me and my friends before or after the services. Sporting his friendly, disarming smile and rosy cheeks, he showed interest and honor to a group of teenagers.

That led me to follow Dr. Stott's writing and ministry, which continue to this day. His character, wisdom, authenticity, and spiritual depth profoundly shaped my understanding of the character of a leader. His theological writing likewise shaped much of my theological understanding. It was clear to me that Dr. Stott's preaching and leadership came from a depth of spiritual development over a lifetime.

At age fifteen, I returned to the United States with my family to finish high school and to attend the University of

Minnesota. Shortly after I returned, Dr. Walter Kaiser Jr., then a professor of Old Testament at Trinity Evangelical Divinity School, came to our church to speak for the weekend. Again, as with Dr. Stott, I was drawn to the depth of character and spiritual understanding that he exhibited.

I was fascinated with Scripture, and especially the Old Testament. I struck up a conversation with Dr. Kaiser, and he became a friend and theological mentor to me through high school and college. When I entered Trinity for my master of divinity, he invited me to become his teaching assistant just as he became dean of the seminary. For four years I worked closely with him, filled in for him in his classes when he was out of town, and helped edit a few of his books. But most significantly, I was deeply imprinted by his character, wisdom, spiritual depth, and leadership ability.

Much of who I am theologically today can be traced to Dr. Kaiser. But far more important, much of who I am as a person and a leader has been influenced by him as well. He was my friend, mentor, supervisor, teacher, and a person of deep influence in my life.

I can name a handful of other individuals who were people of great influence to me. My father; my brother, Tom; my friend of many years, Ken, who is one of the wisest leaders I have met; my brother in Christ, Grant, who thinks more deeply than anyone I have ever met. There is my colleague in ReachGlobal (a global mission), Gary, who asks questions that help clarify issues; Arthur, a person of prayer and spiritual insight; and Wayne, my prayer and travel partner. And of course, Mary Ann, my wife, who has been my best friend now for forty-one years and whose life has impacted mine in ways too numerous to count.

What do all of these individuals have in common? They became people of deep influence to me. They paid the price over a lifetime to cultivate depth in their inner lives, which then overflowed with influence into my life. I am sure that you can identify those of deep influence in your life. They were and are God's gifts to us and deeply influential in who each of us has become. They are Davids, not Sauls, to us.

Join me in the quest to become a leader of deep influence.

For Reflection and Discussion

1. Who were and are the people of deep influence in your life? What was it that made each a person of deep influence to you?

2. What are the ways that you are intentionally building spiritual depth into your life?

3. Which concepts in this chapter caused you to take a second look at your own life?

4. On page 18 is a list of the kinds of habits that characterize people of deep influence. Which of these characterize your life? Which do you need to pay more attention to?

CHAPTER TWO

CHOOSING A POSTURE OF HUMILITY

When building the character of a person of deep influence, humility is the foundation.

I work for a humble leader, and I deeply appreciate that. He has strong opinions and a robust sense of direction. He is willing to listen to others and does not need to be right. He is approachable and reasonable. He hires individuals who are better than he is in their areas of strength, and he leads through a team. Knowing his strengths and his weaknesses, he has built a team to allow him to play to his strengths and to compensate for his weaknesses. His team members are equally strong individuals, none of whom threaten him.

Bill is also confident in who he is and pays close attention to areas where he knows he is vulnerable. On those occasions when I have raised an issue that would have made many leaders uncomfortable, Bill has always listened, always responded thoughtfully, and rarely been defensive. While he is the president of the EFCA and our leader, he shares that leadership willingly and is always ready to share the praise. Ministry is never about him but always about us together.

This describes the healthy understanding of oneself that is a requirement for true humility. Personal insecurities often fuel arrogance as a cover.

I know another leader who also leads a large ministry. He is known to be bright and articulate, but those who have worked for him would not do so again. He is a master at manipulation, believes he is always right, rarely listens to those who push back, and can leave staff members in tears. He communicates that the success of the ministry revolves around him. His leadership style has left people angry, broken, and devastated. Massive arrogance wrapped in a spiritual veneer describes his style. While he has accomplished significant things, it has been at a heavy price for many who were close to him.

Deep influence requires genuine humility. The better the leader, the more humble the leader. This goes to the heart of the leadership role, which is a sacred trust given to a few to further the mission of God's work. King Saul made the mistake of thinking that leadership was about him, rather than a sacred trust. He discovered he was wrong, and God removed him and put into his place a man after God's own heart—David.

Our standard and model was set by Christ Himself:

*In your relationships with one another, have the same
mindset as Christ Jesus:*

Who, being in very nature God,
    did not consider equality with God something to be
        used to his own advantage;
rather, he made himself nothing
    by taking the very nature of a servant,
    being made in human likeness.
And being found in appearance as a man,
    he humbled himself
    by becoming obedient to death—
        even death on a cross!

PHILIPPIANS 2:5-8

Arrogance and entitlement do not yield influence; humility
and other-centered living do!

THE HEART OF HUMILITY

At the heart of humility is an understanding of the twofold
truth that God has given us strengths as a trust and that the
rest of our personal portfolios are made up of weaknesses, for
which we very much need others.

Much of my daily work revolves around writing, whether
my daily blog, books, or material for the organization I lead.
For me, writing is relatively easy: It energizes and fills me.

For most people, writing is a chore and a hassle. I thank God regularly for the gift of writing, which is a trust for me to use on His behalf. It is His gift, so any credit I take is stolen credit. The stronger our gifting, the more credit we owe our Creator, by whom we were "created in Christ Jesus for good works, which God prepared beforehand so that we would walk in them" (Ephesians 2:10, NASB). It is always all about Him!

Humble individuals are deeply aware of their gifting. God gave me the ability to communicate, to develop organizational strategy, and to envision the future. These are strong gifts. But the source of those gifts is Christ. I am deeply thankful for how God gifted and wired me, but for me to take credit for those gifts is to delude myself. He is the source. False humility downplays strengths rather than recognizing them. Genuine humility recognizes those strengths as well as the source and purpose of the strengths.

Humble individuals are *equally* aware of their deficits and weaknesses. Each of us has a few strengths and a multitude of weaknesses. That is why we need others around us who, in playing to *their* strengths, can make up for *our* deficits, and we theirs. The best leaders intentionally build leadership teams in which members play to their strengths; the leaders ensure that their areas of weakness are covered by others.

One of my key partners is Gary. While I can envision the future and develop organizational strategy, I am not great at working the process to get there. Gary is a master at process. Without Gary, my leadership would be much less effective.

Without him and the other individuals on my senior leadership team, ReachGlobal would not be what it is.

Leaders who try to go it alone delude themselves into thinking that they are good enough by themselves to accomplish the mission God has given them. I have met some of those leaders. Usually they could be called arrogant. Mostly people don't like to work directly for them. They may have authority, but they do not lead out of deep influence and often garner more fear than respect.

The heart of humility is recognition that whatever strengths I have were entrusted to me by my Creator to use on His behalf. It is the realization that in my leadership role I deeply *need* others and that it is *we together* who allow me to lead well. In other words it is *not about me!* When Paul told us, "Do not think of yourself more highly than you ought, but rather think of yourself with sober judgment" (Romans 12:3), he was speaking to this truth. It is not a denial of our abilities but a recognition that those abilities are a trust and that we need one another.

We often make too much of a distinction between leaders and those they lead—as if the leader is a more valuable player than the individual who works in the trenches. Here is the truth: The only difference between the leader and the individual on the line is a matter of *gifting*. Without the person in the trenches the leader would have nothing to lead, and without the leader the person in the trenches would not have the guidance and empowerment that makes the organization healthy. Both need one another, both are equally critical players, and both have been divinely gifted by the Creator with different gifts.

This is why it is sinful when leaders do not treat all of those in the organization they lead with honor; they devalue individuals and the gifting God has granted to them.

AUTHENTICITY

Understanding that God has created me with specific gifts, I don't need to pretend that I am better than I am, that I have answers I don't have, or that I don't struggle with weaknesses. At the same time, I don't need to downplay the gifting God has given. He gives only good gifts, and He gives them to be used fully for His kingdom.

Insecure leaders feel a need to appear that they have it all together and know all the answers. The cost is significant emotional pain and anxiety since the facade does not match reality. Humble leaders feel no need to pretend they are something they are not, and they readily admit they don't have all the answers. In fact, they don't need to have the answers because they love to bring people together to find the answers.

This is all about learning to live with personal authenticity. A life of authenticity is rooted in the humility that comes from understanding who we are and who we are not and having no need to pretend we are something we are not. It is a refreshing, what-you-see-is-what-you-get kind of life and leadership.

Authentic leaders, like my leader Bill, garner deep respect.

There is a "realness" to them that attracts. Those who lead out of insecurity, who pretend they are something they are not or lead from authority rather than from influence, are seen for who they are. They may not see their own sad condition, but those who work for them ultimately do. Authentic leaders conduct themselves simply as the men or women that God made them to be and lead out of that authenticity.

Authenticity is a powerful magnet. Authentic leadership is without pretense; it's leading from personal health. And there are not two of me—a public me and a private me—just me. Authentic individuals cultivate healthy spiritual, emotional, and relational practices so that what overflows from their lives is the natural overflow of who they really are. As Jesus said, what is in our hearts is what flows out of us (see Matthew 7:15-23). The key to authenticity is the hidden work a leader does to grow and feed his or her inner life so that its *overflow* is healthy, consistent, and authentic.

Authentic leaders have enough self-assurance that they do not need to foster a persona. Their self-disclosure encourages others to be self-disclosing. They manifest a realness that influences others to be real in return. They are open in a way that creates an open culture, inviting honest dialogue and interaction. People can relate to authenticity. They cannot relate to manufactured personas. Leaders who hide behind personas end up hurting their leadership, while those who cultivate personal authenticity grow their leadership. Authenticity is about humility—being willing to be who we are and to disclose who we are in a healthy, open fashion.

CULTIVATING HUMILITY

Those who experience leadership success run the risk of starting to believe their own press. After all, if I can make such successful ministry calls and grow a church, team, or organization, I must be pretty good. And the better I think I am, the less likely I am to nurture and guard a humble spirit, which is at the core of leaders of deep influence. How do we guard a humble heart?

First, as we've already noted, always remember that our leadership is not about us: Each of us who leads plays a stewardship role. We steward the mission of the organization, the people who work with us (not for us), the strategies that will get us to success, and the resources that are entrusted to us. As soon as we start to believe that the cause is about us, our leadership capital starts to dry up.

Second, surround yourself with competent people who will tell you the truth and will freely share their points of view. Leaders are in a naturally precarious position. Many people will not tell leaders their honest thoughts. They've been conditioned by the many leaders who dislike bad news, who even actively work to stifle honest opinions. The result is that we often do not hear what we need to hear. Wise leaders develop an ethos of candid conversation with those close to them, as well as throughout the organization. Sometimes honest feedback does not feel good, especially from people who are unloving in their critique, but the alternative is a dearth of wisdom.

Here is where insecure leaders flounder. Because they see

dissent, criticism, or contrary opinions as personal attacks, they stifle honest, open dialogue. Some actually respond in anger when contrary opinions are voiced. In shutting down conversation, they lose the intellectual capital of others and don't hear what they really need to hear. This is a net loss for the organization and an indication that the leader thinks everything is about him or her, not about the mission.

I was once tasked to solve a difficult financial issue, and when I presented my findings and solutions to my ministry leader, he became angry and defensive and called me arrogant. Why? Because he did not want to hear bad news that challenged his paradigm of how things "should" be. With a response like that, he was training his people not to give him honest feedback.

This raises a question for leaders: Can I overcome my fear of hearing something that I may not want to hear, and do so in a way that invites honest feedback, rather than pushing it away? The reason we defensively resist honest feedback is that we are fearful that it reflects poorly on us. In Proverbs, it is the fool who resists counsel, while the wise person invites it and listens to it (see Proverbs 15:12; 19:20).

This raises a second question: Why would I risk the danger of not knowing what people really think by resisting honest feedback? The end result of defensiveness is that people often stop telling us what they really think, and only say what they think we want to hear.

There are two predictable outcomes from this scenario. One is that we proceed in ignorance of what is going on within our own team or organization. And the second is that we provoke cynicism from people who do not feel they can be honest. Both are dangerous for a leader.

Humble and healthy leaders want and solicit honest feedback so they can lead well for the health of the organization. Their emotional health and personal security invite honest conversation, and they keep their anxiety and fear under control so that they are open to suggestions and critique. They listen carefully and then evaluate the information for its truth or relevancy. They don't need to agree with the feedback, but they do want to know what people are thinking.

LISTENING AND HUMILITY

A third way to cultivate humility is to listen a lot more than you talk. Insecure leaders talk. A lot. They need to convince themselves and others that they have what it takes to lead, although no one is fooled by their verbosity. Some time ago I had lunch with a new CEO of a major Christian agency of which our organization was a member. In a two-hour lunch this CEO talked about himself continuously. I walked away thinking, "He is not going to last long because he has made everything about him, not about those he is serving." Within two years he was released from his position.

Listening carefully to others is both a posture and a builder of humility. It says, "I want to hear what you are thinking because you are valuable to this organization." It indicates an other-focus rather than selfishness. It sends a loud message that the process is about *us*, not me. I frequently talk to staff of Christian organizations who tell me that staff meetings are taken up with their leader talking to them rather than listening to them. This is not a posture of humility. Those who talk more than listen often do not know what is brewing or what people are thinking—a dangerous situation for all concerned. Those who listen well are far more likely to lead well than those who don't.

In our organization one of our values is that no issue is out of bounds for discussion as long as the dialogue involves no personal attacks or hidden agendas. We don't want any elephants in the room—obvious, oppressive problems that everyone complicitly ignores. At one meeting early in my leadership of ReachGlobal I was told that there were many elephants in the room, so I simply said, "Name them." The thing about elephants is that, once you name them, they are not elephants anymore but simply issues to be discussed. That was not an enjoyable meeting because it included some critical spirits, but we demonstrated that no issues were out of bounds for discussion.

I am fully aware that many people will not tell me what they honestly think because I am the senior leader. I go out of my way with my closest staff to ask them to keep me informed of what is going on in the organization—realities that I would not know without someone telling me. They become my eyes and ears and act as an early warning system when something is brewing and needs attention. They will often coach me on ways that I might mitigate organizational issues. I would rather know the problematic news than not know and be caught by surprise.

The fourth way to cultivate humility is related to the third: Ask a lot of questions of a lot of people. We must do more than remain passively open to feedback; we must actively pursue it. The best leaders I know cultivate the art of asking questions. They are curious; they want to get into the heads of others. They want to learn and to gain different perspectives. Asking questions sends a dual message: "I don't have all the answers, and you are needed." Ironically, many leaders think that asking questions is a sign of weakness, but it takes a strong, self-defined, and personally secure leader to ask questions. This relieves a leader of the burden of pretending he or she has all the answers. It communicates that he or she is willing to be challenged by others.

Questions also work exceedingly well when one is being challenged or even attacked. Rather than bite back and escalate the situation, use questions to engage the individual and to deescalate the conflict. Saying "Talk to me about that" or "Unpack that for me" or "Help me understand your view on that" engages the other individual and keeps a relational connection, rather than cutting off the conversation with a rebuttal.

This is where internal self-discipline matters. Emotionally we may be ready to take a big swipe, claws extended. And the individual may deserve it. But wise leaders censor their responses in order to manage what could otherwise be a problematic conversation.

Openness to and active pursuit of information is difficult and often painful, but the benefit is huge: truthful knowledge. Most of us believe we know more than we actually do—a dangerous misconception. In fact, the greater our ability, the greater the risk that we confuse what we know with what we think we know and underestimate what we don't know. Wise leaders engage others in robust dialogue to test what they think they know, in order to either verify their thinking or to find alternate solutions. Their history of making good decisions may seem brilliant, but if you peel back the process you realize that they did not make them in a vacuum but engaged other bright people in the process.

A test of humility is how often a leader admits that he or she doesn't have the answer to an issue. Those who always have an answer are either fooling themselves or trying to fool others. Those who regularly engage others to find answers are not only humble but are demonstrating authenticity, personal security, and emotional health. Ironically, it is leaders who admit they need help who are more respected than those who pretend or believe they have it all together. The latter pay dearly for their foolishness.

Leaders who believe that they must have the answer and that their internal compass is always right do not solicit feedback or wisdom from others—or they seek feedback only from those they know will agree with them. The go-it-alone style of such leaders often gets them into trouble. In a world of possible solutions to a problem, they are stuck in the small prison of what they actually know—or think they know.

Humble and healthy leaders do not assume they can figure out the right course by themselves. They are by nature desirous of knowing how others are dealing with a problem or opportunity. They do not doubt their ability to get to where they need to go in the end, but they are humble enough to realize that in the world of possible solutions, they know only a few. And if there is a "game-changing" solution, they want to know about it.

For this reason humble leaders rarely make quick decisions but tend to "think gray." This is the ability to hold various points of view and perspectives in tension with one another until an obvious solution emerges. In contrast, prideful leaders often copy someone else's solution (which they may not understand in the least because they lack the originator's process and context).

The more we understand what we don't know, the more open we are to soliciting the input and wisdom of others. The more we do so, the better our own leadership and decision making. Wisdom does not come to the insecure and prideful, but to the secure and humble.

SERVICE AND HUMILITY

The fifth way to cultivate humility: Serve those who serve you. Leaders of deep influence serve those on their teams and help them become the best that they can be as individuals, professionals, and contributors to a common mission. We will only be as good as the teams we lead, so helping them live up to their potential is foundational to our leadership.

As Jesus said,

> *The kings of the Gentiles lord it over them; and those*
> *who exercise authority over them call themselves*
> *Benefactors. But you are not to be like that. Instead,*
> *the greatest among you should be like the youngest,*
> *and the one who rules like the one who serves. For who*
> *is greater, the one who is at the table or the one who*
> *serves? Is it not the one who is at the table? But I am*
> *among you as one who serves.*
> LUKE 22:25-27

Some leaders make it clear that those who work for them are there to serve *them*. Wise, humble leaders go out of their way to serve, grow, and build up those who serve on their teams. It goes back to the distinction that my leadership is not about *me* but about *us* and *the mission* we serve together.

In serving those who work with us, we demonstrate to them that service is at the core of leadership. If I can help my team be successful, I know that the mission will be accomplished. As I demonstrate humble leadership, I establish an ethos of servant leadership for my team. As I demonstrate that life is not about me (a novel concept in our day), I help others realize that life is not about them either: It is about God and the mission He has given us to fulfill.

Serving others well is the antidote to the selfishness of our sinful nature and the pull of a world that says, "It is all about me." As a leader I need to constantly ask the following questions:

- How well am I serving those on my team?
- Do my team members get what they need from me?
- Am I removing barriers that only I as a leader can remove?
- Am I giving staff adequate time and attention and encouragement?
- Do staff clearly understand my expectations so they can be successful?
- Do I go out of my way to solicit and listen to their concerns and ideas?
- Do I take the time just to be "with them" in ways that let them know I care about their lives?

Staying connected, showing genuine concern, and expressing thanks appropriately mean a lot. People want to know that they are respected and appreciated, and that their leader is more than just their boss. It is people who make ministry possible!

Too often leaders who are experiencing success move away from staying close to and serving those they lead. They encounter the temptation to move toward their private priorities rather than continuing to lead the team. After all, they are now *important* and *influential!* This results in a loss of leadership capital as their key team members come to feel abandoned or undervalued. As long as we lead others, the mission we serve and the people we serve must be our highest work-related priorities. When success breeds distance, we lose points and can eventually lose our ability to lead because our leadership withdrawals outweigh our deposits. The greater our success, the more we must guard our personal commitment to those we lead.

Inherent in serving others is the creation of an egalitarian ethos where all members are invited to the idea table, all are seen as valuable members of the team, and all are deeply appreciated for their contributions. Many of those who faithfully serve our organizations at lower levels on the organizational chart are the most valuable people we have. In our organization I think of the women in the donor services department, who input with precision and efficiency every check that comes into our office, often praying for the donors they are serving. What would we do without their service? Do they know how much we appreciate them?

I once had a team member who was an expert in relating well to those above him but disempowering in his relationships with his peers and, even worse, with those who fell "below" him on the organizational chart. His lack of regard for and service to those at his level and below not only led to his departure but caused the department he led to be seen as arrogant and non-service-oriented. While he was competent at what he did, his lack of service was his undoing.

How well I serve those I lead is a barometer of a heart of humility. It is also through my service that I cultivate humility.

LEADING GENEROUSLY

Humble leaders are willing to give opportunity away to others and platform *them* for success, while pride-filled leaders keep opportunity from others and platform *themselves* for success. Not only do humble leaders not care who gets the credit (because everything is about the mission), but they are generous in giving credit to others who have contributed to the success of the mission. They possess an inner security that understands the role they play, and their self-worth is not dependent on being in the spotlight. Ironically, those who crave the credit are seen as selfish and self-centered (and they are), while those who give it away are respected and esteemed for their generosity.

Humble leaders are far more likely to build healthy teams than those who crave the spotlight because they understand their need for others, are willing to share the credit, and love to empower people. Remember, the core of humility is understanding our own strengths and acknowledging them as gifts from God, coupled with our deep need for others to compensate for our many weaknesses. By definition, humble leaders build empowered teams, on which all members play to their strengths and all share the credit for success.

Insecure leaders often build teams as well, but they don't empower those teams and often dominate or control members of the team rather than releasing them. When success comes, it is they who receive the accolades rather than the team together. Why? They are not secure in themselves and long for the applause of others to assure themselves of their personal worth and success! The emotional intelligence of the leader determines whether he or she can lead from a humble posture. (More on emotional intelligence in chapter 6.)

An important question to ask ourselves is, How do I get my significance? Do I get my significance through positive strokes from others (a sign of insecurity), by taking the credit (another sign of insecurity), or by accomplishing the mission, regardless of how many strokes I received or who received the credit (a sign of security)? Understanding our own emotional needs and how our needs impact our leadership for good or ill is an important growth point for each of us. The healthiest leaders are driven by maximizing their influence—no matter what title they have or what credit they receive—and by accomplishing the task God has given the team or organization they lead. If we receive our cookies from unhealthy places, we need to retrain our emotional needs so they are consistent with health.

Many times our craving for significance hurts us because others read our need and tell us what we want to hear ("Pastor, that was the best message I have ever heard"), rather than giving us honest feedback. Healthy leaders do their best, but they want to improve and therefore prefer honest feedback from those they trust. I regularly discount praise from those I don't know or trust—regardless of what I want to hear—because I don't know how objective it is.

I often spend time with organizational staff who feel neglected by otherwise healthy leaders. The leaders are so busy meeting the needs of others that they neglect to nurture their most important constituency—the members of their own teams. They unintentionally send the message that staff are not important, which disempowers members of their team. This is one of the reasons that I regularly ask those who report to me, "What do you need from me?" It is not unusual for them to respond, "T. J. time," which means enough time with their leader that they feel connected and understand what I am thinking and doing so that they can stay in sync.

A key to humble leadership is understanding how our leadership style impacts those around us and working intentionally to ensure that our behaviors empower and honor rather than disempower and dishonor our colleagues. This takes regular reflection on our part, as well as the feedback we solicit from those we lead.

Humility is about generous rather than selfish leadership. Generous leadership honors others, while selfish leadership honors oneself.

DEEP INFLUENCE AND HUMILITY

There is an intrinsic connection between being a person of deep influence and having a heart of humility. People may follow leaders who are arrogant and selfish, especially if it gives them access to power or privilege. However, they respect those who lead out of humility. As Jesus said in His dialogue with the disciples about what it meant to be great in the world compared to what it meant to be great in His kingdom: One was about power; the other was about service (see Luke 22:25-27).

There has been no one more influential in our world than Christ, and He clearly did not fit the world's profile of the powerful. The teachers of the Law and the Pharisees did fit that profile, but Jesus in His humble way confounded them all! There was nothing weak in His humility. He demonstrated humility in love, kindness, openness, care, truth, grace, self-definition, dependence on His Father, and great inner strength. The truth is that healthy and humble people are far stronger than unhealthy and self-centered people. Strength must be projected by the latter, but it flows naturally from the former.

Why did people flock to Jesus? They saw in Him one who was authentic, who loved them, who extended them grace, and who at the same time spoke truth to them. He was a magnet for those who wanted truth and an obstacle for those who resisted truth. He was a person of deep influence who led out of that influence.

Think for a moment of those you most admire and those who have made the most profound impact for good in your life. How did they impact you? Through positional authority? Through power? Or through influence? My guess is that it was through influence. The life of deep influence is the strongest leadership we could ever have, for it mirrors the life of Jesus. It is nurtured constantly with personal humility.

For Reflection and Discussion

1. Where are you most vulnerable to pride and arrogance, and how do you guard yourself against these tendencies?

2. On page 38 we talked about the things we should ask ourselves about how we lead our staff. Which of these are you doing well? Which do you need to pay more attention to?

3. How well does your team or organization reflect a humble posture, and what organizational practices protect this? What additional practices would deepen a posture of humility?

4. What do you do in order to intentionally deepen your personal humility?

CHAPTER THREE

SUFFERING AND LEADERSHIP

I experienced my first real failure at age twenty-eight. My dreams were broken, the vision for my life in shambles. I had resigned from my church after four years of deep pain, had no idea what I would do next, and was suffering from clinical depression. What I did not know then was that my "failure" would be used by God to mold, direct, soften, and sharpen me. He would forge my heart in ways that are impossible except through pain.

It was not a fair suffering! What I have learned over the years is that "fairness" is not God's greatest concern for our lives. His greater concern is that we become who He wants us to be for the sake of what He wants us to do. Life was not fair for Moses, Joseph, Paul, Jesus, David, Esther, or any of the great characters of Scripture. Living in a world undone by sin guarantees that life will not be fair.

There is nothing like pain to test our souls, to forge our character, to help us trust God in the midst of suffering, and to cause us to press into Him when there is no one else to press into. Pain—from any source—is a focusing agent. As a young leader I did not realize the cost of leadership in terms of suffering and pain. As an older leader I realize that the lessons learned in that experience would not have been learned in any other way. Suffering is both the cost of leadership and a prerequisite for becoming a leader of deep influence. There is no other way.

As I survey my life over the past thirty years, I can trace all the major themes of my life to periods of deep pain. It was in those times that God did the most to forge character, faith, heart, soul, and mind. I would not willingly choose to repeat those episodes, but neither would I trade them for anything. As one who wants to exercise deep influence, I can say with honesty, *Thank You, God, for the pain I have endured. You used it to make me who I am.*

NO EASY ROUTES TO DEEP INFLUENCE

A sage of the faith once wrote, "It is doubtful whether God can bless a man greatly until He has hurt him deeply."[1] This is not a statement about God's character but about what it takes to mold our character. A reflection on the great men and women of Scripture reveals periods of great pain and brokenness that shaped them. One of the prices for developing great influence is the experience of suffering.

Peter, speaking to those who were suffering because of their faith, put suffering into an eternal perspective: "Now for a little while you may have had to suffer grief in all kinds of trials. These have come so that the proven genuineness of your faith—of greater worth than gold, which perishes even though refined by fire—may result in praise, glory and honor when Jesus Christ is revealed" (1 Peter 1:6-7).

Suffering, according to Peter, is not a random event but is intimately connected to what God wants to do in our lives—to refine our faith and make us the kind of people who are genuine and pure, which in turn results in praise, glory, and honor to God. There is an authenticity to the faith of those who have gone through deep waters and who, refusing to abdicate to bitterness and a diminished life, follow even harder after God. They trust Him when it makes no human sense to trust. They learn His sufficiency in their pain.

Paul understood the deep connection between understanding Jesus and suffering. He wrote, "I want to know Christ—yes, to know the power of his resurrection and participation in his sufferings, becoming like him in his death, and so, somehow, attaining to the resurrection from the dead" (Philippians 3:10-11).

To know Jesus is first to understand what it means to be "a man of sorrows, acquainted with deepest grief" (Isaiah 53:3, NLT). While health, wealth, and prosperity are proclaimed today as God's will for all of His people, Scripture says that those who suffer share in the fellowship of Christ's sufferings. The book of Hebrews encourages us with the truth that "Son though he was, he learned obedience from what he suffered and, once made perfect, he became the source of eternal salvation for all who obey him" (Hebrews 5:8-9). If the very Son of God was molded by suffering, how can any of His followers assume that they might escape the same molding process?

Without the dark nights of the soul, David would never have been able to write the Psalms, the passages to which all of us turn when we suffer our dark nights of the soul. Without his wilderness experience, Moses would never have become God's most humble leader, with whom He spoke face-to-face. Without Abraham's willingness to follow God in faith he would never have become the paradigm of faith for all the generations after him. Without suffering, the Messiah would not have become the bearer of our sin!

When all is said and done, God is more concerned about the refining of our faith and lives than He is about our comfort and ease. The picture that Peter uses of faith "refined by fire" is the picture of the heating of metals in the forge so that the dross floats to the surface and can be scraped off and thrown out, leaving something pure and beautiful behind. Pain and suffering do for our hearts what the fire does for precious metals. There is no other way to purify metal, and there is no other way to purify our hearts.

THE PERSPECTIVE OF SUFFERING

When I packed my truck on a blistering hot September day in 1986 to leave my pastorate, I had no money, no job waiting, and no hope. I was devastated, sad, tired, and depressed and had a lot of questions for God, for which I was receiving no answers. My name and reputation were being trashed; I had to leave my reputation with God. I was in survival mode, unable to see beyond the pain. I was simply hanging on to God, and that is all. I manifested no great faith, harbored no assumption of what He would do. I was just trying to survive my faith.

I now have the perspective of twenty-five-plus years. It was through that pain that my theology of grace grew to become a lifestyle of grace, in which I no longer needed to prove myself to God or others. It was because of those circumstances that I ended up at the national office of the EFCA, which led to my greatest life convergence. It was through my dark night of the soul that I birthed five books and started to consult with church boards and staff on healthy leaders, intentional leadership, and empowered structures.

Through the tough days I learned that God would be faithful if I would just trust Him. I let go of my need for "justice" (sometimes vengeance) and left that burden with Him. My depression led me to counseling and medication, which in turn gave me empathy for those who suffer from emotional pain on a regular basis. Slowly over time the pain gave way to mercy, grace, and a spiritual perspective. Memories that once tied my stomach in knots for days became mere parts of my biography, informing who I am today. Over time my experience of pain turned from that of hopelessness and suffering to that of God's gracious grace, which forged a more perfect me—the *me* God designed me to be.

I wrote in chapter 1 that God is not in a hurry. We often are, but He never is. He is on a deliberate path to mold the me that He made me to be, and He is far more concerned *that* I get there than *when* I get there. We often see periods of pain and suffering as setbacks and time-outs. They never are for God; they are a deliberate part of His plan to mold us for the unique work He has for us, whether as a leader or for any other role.

On December 4, 2007, I went into the emergency room for what would end up being a forty-three-day hospital stay, thirty-five days in the ICU hovering between life and death from MRSA pneumonia and numerous complications. I was only three and a half years into my new leadership assignment at ReachGlobal. The health crisis took me out of the game for six months while I tried to recover my strength.

Wasted time? The lessons that God taught me in those months could fill a journal. Lessons that could not be learned any other way, lessons about faith, prayer, grace, healing, and God's amazing graciousness. And in slowing down my body for much of a year, He gave me the time to write *Live Like You Mean It* and *When Life Comes Undone* to influence others to live at the intersection between our relationship with Him and His call on our lives. The lessons learned in that time of suffering will inform each day of the remainder of my life, and many have commented on how it changed me! As leaders, we above all thank Him for the hard times because those times mold us most profoundly and make us the best leaders.

SUFFERING AND FREEDOM

All of us have issues! We have dysfunctions and insecurities, and we are bound up by our own expectations or the expectations of others. One of the greatest gifts of suffering is its ability to move us toward personal freedom, bringing the dross—the dysfunctional and unhealthy—to the surface in the forge and bit by bit spooning it onto the garbage heap.

I am by nature a driven individual. I had also been pretty successful at anything I put my hand to, and until the age of twenty-eight I had never failed at anything. Before seminary I had preached in one hundred churches and had been president of my youth group and of my InterVarsity chapter at the University of Minnesota. In seminary I served as the dean's teaching assistant. Failure was not something I was acquainted with—until, as a pastor, I ran into the sharp teeth of the buzz saw.

That failure was the start of a journey toward greater personal freedom and toward the *me* that God had created me to be. The day I left town in a truck stuffed to the gills with all my books—and with a new, unappreciated life experience under my belt—I had gained a freedom that I didn't at the time understand. How many of us live with fear of failure? Well, I had failed and survived, so I no longer needed to fear failure. Freedom.

When I decided not to take another church in the aftermath of my dark night of the soul—I knew I was not ready—I had to face the expectations of others about what I would do with my life. I engaged in a few heated discussions with my father and others. But once I had battled through those expectations, I gained new freedom. I could be just who God wanted me to be!

Think about these freedoms that arise from hardship:

- Once humbled, we no longer need to worry about our pride.
- Once having failed, we no longer need to fear failure.
- Once we have let others down, we no longer need to worry about their expectations.
- Once we've found ourselves in need of God's grace, we no longer need to pretend we have it all together.
- Once we've been broken, we carry a more mature perspective into our next brokenness experience.
- Once we've had to bet it all on Jesus, we know that we can do it again and He will again prove trustworthy.
- Once our reputation has been trashed, we learn that we can leave it in the hands of God.
- Once we've faced injustice, we are free to leave justice with Him.
- Once we've faced our great depravity, we allow His grace to wash through our lives with joy.

Given the choice between suffering, together with the freedom it can bring, and a life of comfort, along with the bondage of my baggage, I would choose suffering and freedom any day. Suffering is a prerequisite to becoming a person of deep influence and a by-product of the same. Suffering creates better leadership, and good leadership inevitably creates suffering as some of the sheep choose not to follow but to bite back.

All suffering creates a dilemma for us. Do we push away from God in bitterness, in our pain and unanswered questions, or do we push harder into God in spite of our questions and pain? One path leads to bitterness toward God and a diminished life, the other toward freedom and a more faithful life. On the day I left town from my pastorate I made a choice. I was confused, I was wounded beyond belief, and nothing seemed fair. But I *chose* to trust God. It was not an easy choice. And it wasn't a choice I could afford to postpone; I had to make it in the midst of the pain. In the light of many more years' maturity, I see the wisdom of the choice.

Pain and suffering force us to ask hard questions that we otherwise would not ask, and to resolve them one way or the other. They are the questions and issues that in good times we can ignore or push aside; but in hard times we must confront them head on.

I was forced to confront such a question in January 2009 (a second ICU stay), lying in a hospital bed in Bangkok, Thailand, on a ventilator, having multiple antibiotics pumped into my body, my system fighting massive pneumonia, septic shock, and acute respiratory distress syndrome. I was teetering on the edge between life and death. To complicate matters this was the second such session in the hospital in the course of a year, and the prognosis was not good.

Because I was not sedated, I had a lot of time to think. Where does one turn when there are no other options? Questions burned in my mind. Is God truly good? Is He enough? Is He still good if I do not survive this battle? Messages I had preached and pieces I had written were parsed in my brain as I considered ultimate questions that ultimate situations force one to ask. There is a great difference between asking such questions in the quiet of my study, sitting in my leather chair surrounded by my commentaries, and asking them in the stark reality of an ICU in a foreign country, my wife in the United States and medical indicators in free fall.

I came to settle on several truths, which I forced my mind around time after time when the uncertainty and pain threatened to overwhelm me. First, the most repeated command in Scripture is to not be afraid (see Joshua 1:9; Matthew 14:27). Second, God's often repeated promise is that He is with us (see Psalm 23; Matthew 28:20). And third, my conviction, shaped through previous suffering, is that God is good—all the time (see Psalm 36:5-9; Romans 8:28-39). I also concluded that it is a wonderful gift to come to the place where one's only recourse is to turn to God, because in *that* place we find that He is indeed sufficient—all that we ultimately need.

There is no greater freedom than to learn such ultimate lessons in our bones and not simply in our minds. I know that I have looked death square in the face twice and that He has been faithful in both instances. And I know that He would have been just as faithful even if I had not survived. That's freedom.

THE SUFFERING INHERENT IN MYSTERY

Christian leadership is not for the faint of heart. We are confronted each day with disappointments and challenges that test our faith, our trust, and our view of God's divine sovereignty and goodness. It is one thing to proclaim God's answers to others. It is another to wrestle with them ourselves.

A good friend dies. Another discovers she has cancer. A ministry plan goes askew. We are attacked by someone who should know better. I am talking about the issues that tear at our hearts and cause us consciously or unconsciously to doubt the very God we serve and proclaim. For ministry leaders the pain can get very personal.

We may not admit the truth even to ourselves, but disillusionment with God is not uncommon among ministry leaders. And when it comes, it is often accompanied by an underlying anger that spills over in unexpected ways, onto unsuspecting people. Our personal issues with God become toxic as we struggle with the disconnect between our theology and painful personal experience. From this dissonance flows a poisonous mix of anger and bitterness. After all, there is no anger more personal than anger at God—anger that He allows or even causes circumstances that we believe He should not.

This is a dangerous moment for leaders because the

relentless undercurrent of anger hurts those we lead, and our followers end up walking on eggshells around us. Where can we go for restoration in those situations? We go back to five basic truths and principles that must drive our spiritual leadership and must be the presuppositions from which we think, live, and minister. These core truths are what help us move *toward* God rather than *away* from Him when suffering comes our way.

One: God is good all the time, even though we live in a fallen world. We can always count on His goodness; we must trust in it, for if God is not good, nothing proclaimed in Scripture about Him can be trusted (see Romans 8:28-39; Psalm 23).

Two: God's goodness does not prevent us from suffering. Indeed, we share in the fellowship of His sufferings (see Philippians 3:10), and our scars become trophies if we trust Him in the midst of our pain.

Three: God's ways are indeed inscrutable to human eyes— majestic, eternal, sovereign, and divinely good in ways that we cannot understand this side of eternity (see Romans 9; Job 38-42).

Four: God has an eternal prevent in all things that transcends our limited understanding. That purpose is good and will be fulfilled as the glory of God becomes known across our globe. Often failure and pain are the antecedents to amazing glory and eternal success (see Isaiah 40).

Five: We play a humble part in God's eternal purposes and cannot take personal responsibility for the completion of His plan. When we carry a burden of responsibility that He was meant to carry, we become weary, disillusioned, and often angry. We must leave His purposes and His burdens in His hands and watch Him unfold His inscrutable plan through us (see Ephesians 2:10).

In the ancient world when armies went to battle, the goal of the opposing side was to put an arrow into the heart of the king leading the battle. The same is true in the spiritual battle today. Ministry leaders become the targets of those who are unhappy from within the ranks or from outside. The leaders often unfairly take the brunt of attack for their leadership. That is when it is critical to understand that the battle is not about us but about the mission we serve and the One we serve. We take arrows on His behalf. It is part of the stewardship of leadership and of sharing in the fellowship of His sufferings.

WHEN THE SHEEP BITE

In his qualifications for overseers or elders, Peter gave a crucial requirement—that shepherds serve "not because you must, but because you are willing, as God wants you to be" (1 Peter 5:2). Why is it so critical that leaders serve willingly? I believe it is because those nice, furry, soft, gentle-looking sheep have minds of their own, and they may even bite the hand that feeds them.

Some of the most painful seasons for Christian leaders come when they've been shot at from within their own camp. When the sheep bite, our natural tendency is to kick back—hard—but that is exactly what a faithful shepherd does not do. Leaders who serve out of obligation are far more likely to kick back than those who have counted the cost and have chosen to lead in spite of the sacrifices inherent in the job.

I did not leave my church because of outside difficulties but because of a few insiders who wanted me to go. My pain was not from the pagans in the community but the saints in the pew. It came at a time when the church was experiencing significant growth; individuals were coming to Christ regularly, and lives were being significantly changed. My situation was far from unique; it happens every day in the bride of Christ, to the chagrin and pain of the One who died for the bride. But it is the consequence of living and ministering in a fallen world.

In the wake of many years of ministry I can say with conviction that God is fair; fairness is part of His character. I can also say with clarity that people and circumstances of life are not! And that one of the burdens of serving Christ is the willingness to accept that unfairness for the sake of the One we serve and for the cause He represents.

Jesus told His disciples, "If the world hates you, keep in mind that it hated me first. If you belonged to the world, it would love you as its own. As it is, you do not belong to the world, but I have chosen you out of the world. That is why the world hates you" (John 15:18-19).

In his farewell to the elders at Ephesus, Paul reminded those leaders that "even from your own number men will arise and distort the truth in order to draw away disciples after them. So be on your guard!" (Acts 20:30-31).

Herein lies a challenge for those who lead God's people. We choose this ministry because of our love for Him and our desire to point people to Him. We soon discover that some people don't play fair, that ungodly attitudes and actions are ubiquitous even in the church, and that our efforts to shepherd others are often met with resistance. For young leaders this rude awakening can bring periods of great pain, as it did for me. And unfortunately the pain does not cease as the years pass. What can change is our ability to handle the pain inherent in ministry.

It was no different for Christ, whom we serve as undershepherds. He dealt with the sadness of loss and betrayal. At His most painful and crucial hour He was abandoned by those closest to Him (think of Peter's betrayal on the night he was arrested). People to whom He showed compassion walked away, unwilling to pay the price of following Him (see Matthew 19:16-22). When His teaching became hard for them to hear, they abandoned Him in swarms (see John 6:60). His own disciples often did not understand what He said (see Matthew 16:21-23). He was maligned, and His character besmirched (see Matthew 13:53-58). He was targeted by the Evil One with temptation (see Matthew 4:1-11).

I am frequently amused by the long list of potential bad side effects one reads when prescribed new medication. There ought to be mandatory courses on the cost of ministry for all those who are thinking about going into full-time Christian service. Unlike the side effects of medications, which might happen, the side effects of ministry *will* happen.

This is not to discourage would-be Christian workers. I would not choose to do anything else at any price. But I make my choice knowing the cost—and also knowing that this is what Christ has called me to and that my reward will not primarily come in this life: "When the Chief Shepherd appears, you will receive the crown of glory that will never fade away" (1 Peter 5:4). I also know that in the moments of deepest suffering I become the person God meant me to be. Thus I have the privilege of sharing in the fellowship of His suffering, following in His footsteps and becoming more like Him in the hard times. I counsel people not to go into full-time ministry unless they are absolutely sure that is where God is calling them. The cost is high. But the benefits are higher.

Deep influence is about the character that constitutes the foundation of our leadership. The test of our character is not how we respond when times are good but when times are bad; that is when our truest character is revealed. For those who serve as undershepherds it comes down to this: When the chips are down do we preserve or hurt the bride?

I am deeply distressed by the number of pastors and Christian leaders who, when the chips are down, when they are under pressure to leave their ministry, choose to hurt God's work in anger on their way out. Their anger may or may not be justified, but inflicting violence on the bride of Christ, the local church, is never justified.

When we as Christ's leaders fight back—and all of us are tempted to do so—we forget who our audience is. We fight back because we forget that ministry is not about *us* but about *Him*. Our audience is Jesus Himself, and when we hurt His ministry, we dishonor Him.

Paul understood that ultimately he served an audience of one—Jesus Christ—and that he would ultimately answer to only one for his actions: "So we make it our goal to please him, whether we are at home in the body or away from it. For we must all appear before the judgment seat of Christ, so that each of us may receive what is due us for the things done while in the body, whether good or bad" (2 Corinthians 5:9-10). If we suffer, we do so for *Him*. If we respond, we need to do so in a way that pleases and glorifies *Him*, rather than looking after our personal concerns.

SPIRITUAL WARFARE

Often in our suffering we focus on the people who are the visible agents of that suffering rather than on the invisible, spiritual agent who is the ultimate culprit. I am convinced that at least in the West we have a deeply inadequate theology of spiritual warfare, which is being fought in the unseen world around us twenty-four/seven. Many irritating people are simply being used unwittingly by the Evil One to hurt the cause of Christ.

If we could see for just an instant what is going on in the unseen world around us, we would be forever changed. Paul understood that world:

*Finally, be strong in the Lord and in his mighty
power. Put on the full armor of God, so that you can
take your stand against the devil's schemes. For our
struggle is not against flesh and blood, but against
the rulers, against the authorities, against the powers
of this dark world and against the spiritual forces of
evil in the heavenly realms. Therefore put on the full
armor of God, so that when the day of evil comes,
you may be able to stand your ground, and after you
have done everything, to stand.*

EPHESIANS 6:10-13

When we think of suffering and pain in ministry we often
think of those human individuals who have inflicted it on
us. What we forget is that it is not primarily about them but
about the Evil One who will use whatever agents he can find
to hurt the work of God.

Should we be angry at times? Yes! But in most cases our
anger should be directed at the one whose temptation and
lies influence those who hurt us. Our prayers ought to be for
the exposure of truth and falsehood, for protection against
the Evil One, and for victory in the cosmic battle between
the forces of Christ and the forces of Satan.

And should it be any surprise that the commanders in
that battle—those of us in full-time ministry—would be the
primary targets of the Evil One? If he can take us out, discourage us, anger us, hurt us, our leadership ability is compromised. Those on the front lines who are calling the plays

will be the targets—Satan is no fool! What we need is a whole lot of discernment and protection.

For my family, part of that protection comes from three prayer teams—one very intimate team to whom we can tell anything, a second that is told much, and a third that is much larger. My goal is to gather the largest prayer team possible, because I accept the reality of the spiritual forces that I have chosen to confront in my leadership role within a denomination and through the international ministry of ReachGlobal. The greater the vision and commitment, the harder the pushback from the Evil One.

GETTING BACK IN THE GAME

The pain of my own failure and disappointment at age twenty-eight would mark my life for many years, ultimately in good ways. But in the aftermath of my pain I looked for safe places to work and was very cautious about stepping into everything God had made me to be. Through a series of God-orchestrated circumstances I ended up working at the EFCA national office, first as the assistant to the president and then as the executive director of ministry advancement. I also went into counseling and started medication for deep depression. I maneuvered cautiously through leadership and ministry for probably ten years. The pain was too great and my fear of revisiting that pain too deep to plunge boldly ahead.

I started to write and to consult with churches on issues of leadership and governance. During one of those consultations God gave me a gift in the form of a new friend, Arthur

Ellison. Arthur is by gifting a leader, a man of deep prayer, and one who listens well to God.

Arthur asked Mary Ann and me if he could form a personal prayer team for us. He did so, and soon we had a small group of friends who were praying for us on a regular basis. As they prayed, they became convinced that they needed to come and pray for us in person. During that visit to my office they pressed into the pain of my past. They challenged me to once again take the risk to step fully into my gifting (and my wife into hers), to take up the baton of leadership for which God had designed me, and to fulfill God's calling on my life.

As they prayed for me, I remember weeping as the pain of the past washed over me, and God's call beckoned me. I knew that the time had come to step out once again. I knew that I was ready to let go of the pain of the past and embrace the future. I knew that the scars of the past had turned into divine scars, trophies, tools that I could use for His purposes. They were His scars now, not mine.

God used prayer and the ministry of my prayer team to redeem the years that the locusts had eaten, to give me the courage to step more fully into my calling than I had ever done. Since that day, God has led me to write, to teach, to consult, and to lead an international organization that I love, ReachGlobal, which touches more than a hundred countries.

I share these intimate details of our life to encourage those of you who have been wounded or sidelined by the suffering that comes from ministry. It is very real! It can take a great toll on us. But it can also form the deepest part of our spiritual, emotional, and relational lives in ways that allow us to respond to God's call with courage and completeness that would otherwise remain out of reach. I am forever indebted to those friends who came around us to cheer us on and to challenge our faith. They were God's instruments to get us back in the game, helping to transform suffering into part of our eternal legacy for Him.

If you are where I was, will you consider stepping back into your calling and your legacy? Will you consider allowing your scars to become divine scars? Is it time for you?

CHOOSING DIVINE SCARS

All of us have scars from life. At fifty-seven I have many, some self-inflicted, some inflicted by others, some from illness and circumstances beyond my control, some from the leadership positions I have held. The question is not whether we will incur scars but whether we will respond to hurt and suffering in ways that turn those scars into divine scars. Wounds are never pleasant. What we do with the wounds makes all the difference in allowing God to use them to mold us.

With every wound we have a choice: Do we bite back in anger or respond in love? Do we choose bitterness or deeper faith? Do we allow it to diminish our lives or enrich our lives? Every wound, in other words, is an opportunity to build strength, character, resolve, and faith into our lives, or to settle for a diminished life.

Those who are wounded in battle receive medals of honor for their willingness to do the courageous thing in the face of danger. Those leaders who translate their wounds into divine scars can wear those scars as medals of honor in this life and, I am convinced, in eternity. There is a price for leadership, but one day we will "receive the crown of glory that will never fade away" from the One on whose behalf we lead (1 Peter 5:4).

For Reflection and Discussion

1. How would you articulate a theology of pain and suffering?

2. Looking back over your life, how has God used pain and suffering to mold you into who you are today? What lessons did you learn in the process?

3. How has God used suffering to bring you to a place of greater personal freedom?

4. Has pain caused you to live cautiously? Do you need to step fully, once again, into your God-given calling?

5. Who are the people around you who might be able to help you heal from unresolved pain?

CHAPTER FOUR

EMBRACING SPIRITUAL TRANSFORMATION

Deep influence has everything to do with our inner lives. Our influence is not so much about *how* we lead as from what *source* we choose to lead. At its core is our desire to embrace the spiritual transformation Christ wants to bring. The deepest influence is the influence of Christ living in us.

The heart of life with Christ is the fact that in salvation we enter into a very personal relationship with the Lord of the universe, whose very person invades our life through the presence of the Holy Spirit. His goal is to transform our lives, and His method is *Christ in us*, the hope of glory (see Colossians 1:27).

Spiritual transformation leads to changes in our character,

lifestyle, habits, and practices. All too often, however, we have reversed the order, thinking that if we live or act a certain way then we will earn God's pleasure. Just watch new believers as they are coached by other believers in what lifestyle choices they should embrace or avoid. Quickly they are *enculturated* into a lifestyle that *looks* like those around them. What *looks* a certain way on the outside often has *little* to do with true spiritual transformation. Furthermore, real transformation is a work of the Holy Spirit—not the work of other people—as He convicts us of sin, brings us to repentance, and instills new practices that are consistent with the character of God.

Transformation is not about the adoption of a new set of rules and regulations in place of the old set of rules and regulations by which I lived previously. This is a skewed understanding of transformation that was embraced by the Pharisees, who substituted outward regulations for inner transformation.

Transformation is the process by which God, through His Holy Spirit and with our active cooperation, brings change to our lives, as we allow Him to realign our lives with His. It is a deeply personal process that impacts our hearts, our minds, our priorities, and our relationships. There is *no* part of our lives that God does not want to infuse with His life and to transform.

This transformation is at the core of deep influence, because the deepest influence we will ever have comes not out of our wisdom or leadership but from a heart and a mind that have been so transformed by the Holy Spirit that they increasingly reflect the heart and mind of God! This is not primarily about knowing *about* God (although that is important) but *knowing* God and choosing to remain continuously open to His reformation.

WHO DOES GOD WANT US TO BE?

God wants you to be the person He designed and made *you* to be. Paul says in Ephesians 2:10 that "we are His workmanship, created in Christ Jesus for good works, which God prepared beforehand so that we would walk in them" (NASB), indicating that each of us is uniquely designed by God and that no two of us are alike. God designed a unique me, never to be repeated, and a unique you, never to be repeated. We are each one of a kind!

And in His creativity He wired and gifted us for unique purposes—"good works . . . prepared beforehand"—that only we can fulfill. God created me to lead the organization I lead. He created me to write a book called *Deep Influence*. He created me to be a husband of a wonderful woman and the father of two wonderful boys. He created me for a unique work in His kingdom that I am uniquely wired to carry out. And the same is true for every one of us, no matter what our occupation or circumstance.

You and I were created for relationship with Christ, and in Christ we have the two desires of every heart: a desire for relationship (I experience that in Christ and His people), and a desire for significance (leaving an eternal legacy).

When I came to Christ and invited Him into my life, the

unique me that God created me to be did not change. I was hardwired with gifts of vision, strategy, and communication. For everything else, I was not hardwired! When I came to Christ, He took His creation and infused it with His Holy Spirit, forgiving my sin and empowering the wiring He gave me at birth. He then launched me on a journey that the New Testament calls *sanctification*—the lifelong process by which my lower and sinful nature is taken off, piece by piece, and His holy nature is put on, piece by piece.

Many people believe that God wants to turn our lives completely around when we first come to Him. That is a misunderstanding of God's intentions. Many of our *behaviors* will change, and those behaviors need to change 180 degrees. But God wants to take His unique creation and *complete* that creation, which was marred when sin entered our world so many eons ago. His plan is to use time and life experience to shape each of us into the man or woman He made us to be. The process by which we realize the full potential for which we were created is spiritual transformation.

Some fear the process of spiritual transformation, believing erroneously that it will cost them too much. This fear is the manifestation of our old sinful nature's craving for autonomy. Autonomy from God leads us away from God and toward our shadow side. Engaging in humble dependence upon God leads us toward His life and character—and toward deep influence with others.

Some people—even many in ministry—simply do not pay enough attention to this aspect of their lives and end up living at a shallow spiritual level, substituting activity for true life change. This is a trap that prevents them from realizing their full potential or being able to exercise the influence for which God designed them. Shallow spiritual lives lead to shallow influence, even if masked by impressive achievements. There simply is no substitute for going deep with Jesus!

Christ's vision for our lives is very simple: "Do not conform to the pattern of this world, but be transformed by the renewing of your mind. Then you will be able to test and approve what God's will is—his good, pleasing and perfect will" (Romans 12:2). There is a direct connection here between the transforming of our lives, the renewing of our minds, and our ability to understand "God's . . . good, pleasing and perfect will." Making our ongoing inner transformation a life priority is a prerequisite for being people of deep influence.

A real trap for leaders in full-time vocational ministry is to substitute our work *for* God (our ministry) for the work *of* God in our hearts and lives. This substitution hurts us because we then fall short of all that God made us to be. Further, we model to others that ministry is about activity *for* God rather than life *with* God. When this happens, we miss out on the innate joy and reward of a character like Jesus.

I'm not saying that inner transformation excludes outward activity. It's a matter of which one is the central focus. If my priority is submitting to authentic spiritual transformation, the outward behaviors will come naturally: I *will* work to bring all of life under His lordship; I *will* engage in His business; I *will* modify my life in many areas to bring them into alignment with His will. But if instead I focus first on doing things for Him and modifying my behaviors, I will end up trying to prove myself to God—a dysfunction that drives too many Christian leaders.

FOUR KEY AREAS OF TRANSFORMATION

Transformation does not allow for compartmentalization of our lives; we don't get to choose which areas of life we will give to God and which we will keep from Him. Studies show that the lifestyle and priorities of those who label themselves as evangelicals are almost no different from those who don't claim to be Christ-followers. This indicates that a great deal of compartmentalization is taking place.

A Christian who compartmentalizes and holds something back from God goes through a pseudo transformation: Justification (my sins have been forgiven) has not been followed by serious sanctification (my life has been and is being changed). If I choose the areas of my life to which I will grant God access, salvation may well have occurred in me, but the process of my becoming all that God created me to be is circumvented. A divided life brings only frustration.

Authentic transformation involves purposefully inviting God into four areas of our lives. In each of these areas we agree to cooperate with His Spirit's work to become more like Him. These four areas include our *hearts*, our *thinking*, our *priorities*, and our *relationships*. These areas of transformation are keys to the development of deep influence because they impact not only our personal lives but also our leadership practices.

Transformation of Our Hearts

This may seem obvious since giving one's heart to Christ is the key to an eternal relationship with Him. This new life in Christ comes to us, not because of something we have done, but on the basis of God's grace, freely extended to us: "For it is by grace you have been saved, through faith—and this is not from yourselves, it is the gift of God—not by works, so that no one can boast" (Ephesians 2:8-9).

It is God who performs ongoing transformation of our hearts in response to our continued faith. It is all about His grace in our lives. Not only do we enter His kingdom by grace, but we live out our daily lives in His grace, and it is this daily living *in grace* that is perhaps our most difficult challenge.

Grace is defined as unmerited favor. None of us merits the favor of God, "but God demonstrates his own love for us in this: While we were still sinners, Christ died for us" (Romans 5:8). When we were still in rebellion, He moved toward us, became one of us in the incarnation, and died for our sin!

So if God has, at salvation, transformed our hearts through His grace—bringing us into His family, forgiving our sin, giving us an eternal destiny—why do we speak further of the need for transformation of our hearts? I believe the challenge is not in accepting that His grace has forgiven our sin and reconciled us to Him. The challenge is in understanding how His grace impacts our daily life and leadership.

Many of us struggle with a deep feeling of unworthiness

in our relationship with God, and frankly many of us spend our lives trying to make ourselves worthy of Him even after we have accepted His gift of salvation. In our struggle with sin we find ourselves doubting our worthiness. That often leads us to work harder to please Him, thinking that the more we do for Him the more we are worthy of Him. I once thought this way as well; I believed I had something to prove to God.

But here is the catch: There is nothing we can do to cause God to love us more, and there is nothing we can do to cause God to love us less. We live and exist in His pure, unrelenting, and infinite grace. That means we can relax in our relationship with Him. We are worthy of Him because He has made us worthy. We are called His friends and His brothers because He has made us family. When we come to understand His grace, we can stop striving for His love and acceptance because through His grace we live in His love and acceptance all the time.

Why is this so important? The Christian world is full of Christ-followers (and ministry leaders) who are still trying to earn God's love instead of simply living in His wonderful grace. If we know that we don't need to earn His love (it is not possible), we are then able to serve Him with grateful, thankful hearts, without fear, knowing that we exist in His grace *every moment* and that our failures are all covered by grace. The more we understand grace, the more we relax in our relationship with Jesus and the more confidence we have in our personal walk with Him.

Transformation of the heart is therefore crucial—first, for

salvation and entrance into His family and, second, for living every day with confidence, not in ourselves, but in His limitless, empowering grace. None of us will be the man or woman He created us to be until each understands what it means to live daily in His grace. Transformation continues in our hearts as we daily unfold the full implications of the grace we have entered into.

Leaders who do not have a good grasp of the grace of God in their lives often do not extend grace to those they lead. Leaders who are driven to prove something to God often drive those they lead as well. The greater the transformation of my own heart, the more of God's heart I will extend to others.

That is why those who have the greatest spiritual influence are those who are the most comfortable in their relationship with the Father. The more confident a leader is in relationship with God, the more secure he or she is. That inner security is a key component of deep influence because it allows us to live with a nothing-to-prove-nothing-to-lose attitude in our life and leadership. It removes the insecurities that are all too common among Christian leaders.

Transformation of Our Thinking

Paul made a remarkable statement about how he lived life: "We take captive every thought to make it obedient to Christ" (2 Corinthians 10:5). Think about the picture he paints with this metaphor: taking captive—bringing into submission—every thought, to make those thoughts obedient to Christ.

What does it mean to make our *thoughts* obedient to

Christ? The implication is that our thoughts can be either disobedient or obedient! We often think about actions or behaviors that are disobedient or obedient to Christ. But the source of our outward disobedience or obedience lies fundamentally in whether our *thinking* is in sync with Christ.

Taking every thought captive is about intentionally aligning our thinking with how God thinks. It is understanding His concerns and making them our concerns, grasping His priorities and making them our priorities, seeking always to understand how Christ would view the issues we are facing.

I have engaged in leadership dialogues in many countries, and I often receive the response, "But this is how we do it in our country," even when the practices in question conflict with biblical teaching. My standard response is, "There is a way of doing it in your culture and a way of doing it in my culture. But there is also a way of doing it in God's kingdom, and *that* is our central concern, because we are citizens of His kingdom."

One of the reasons that people of deep influence immerse themselves in Scripture is that they understand it is the key to understanding the heart and mind of God. It is the means by which they can align their thinking with God's thinking. Let's revisit Romans 12:2: "Do not conform to the pattern of this world, but be transformed by the renewing of your mind. Then you will be able to test and approve what God's will is—his good, pleasing and perfect will."

If we desire to bring our thinking into alignment with God's values and concerns, we will constantly ask ourselves, What does God have to say about this issue? We will not simply accept the thinking of those around us or the prevailing wisdom of our culture. There is a way of viewing issues in our culture, but we are people of God's culture (His kingdom), and the two are not the same.

The transformations of heart and mind are linked in such a way that our understanding of God's grace motivates us to bring our lives into submission to Him. That submission starts with our minds and an intentional desire to know Him and to understand His heart.

True leaders are naturally on the cutting edge of thinking. It is one of the characteristics of leaders—they spend a lot of time thinking, and they *lead* others to think critically. One of the greatest gifts a leader can give to those he or she leads is the practice of thinking biblically.

Transformation of our minds requires more than a surface reading of Scripture. It takes a thoughtful approach to His truth. We all evaluate issues through a grid that we have acquired, and the more that grid is influenced by our understanding of Scripture, the more it will be influenced by the mind of God. The more we possess of the mind of Christ, the deeper our influence—that is, His influence through us.

Transformation of Our Priorities

Our priorities reveal what is truly important to us, rather than what we *claim* is important to us. And they come from the commitment of our heart and the condition of our mind.

Jesus made an amazing statement in John 6:38, considering that He is one of the three members of the Trinity. He said, "For I have come down from heaven not to do my will but to do the will of him who sent me." Here was Jesus, committed to doing the will of His Father, to be in submission to His Father's will. His highest priority was to do the will of the One who sent Him.

In the same vein, speaking to His disciples He said, "Whoever serves me must follow me; and where I am, my servant also will be. My Father will honor the one who serves me" (John 12:26). For Christ-followers, life is not about us—it is all about Him. To the extent that we believe that life is about *Him* and that we are here to do His will, we will rely on Him to show us what is truly important in our lives.

One of the fundamental decisions each of us makes is whether life is about us or about Christ—whether we will devote ourselves to advancing our own agenda or His agenda in our world. The two choices are mutually exclusive, and our decision will directly determine the influence we have for Him.

Life is a series of choices, and those choices are smaller versions of the bigger question: Is life about me or about God? Even after we have answered that question in its macro form, we face micro versions of the same question each day, each week, each month, each year.

The question of our life agendas is a deeply personal one that requires significant thought and introspection. I know pastors, for instance, whose motivation is all about success as defined by numbers—which looks very much like a personal agenda. I meet other pastors whose motivation is all about helping God's people become all that they can be—which looks very much like God's agenda. Both are involved in God's work, but their priorities are different. It is dangerously easy to engage in full-time ministry with agendas and priorities that are more about us than about God.

As the leader of an international ministry, I am always faced with the personal question, Is this about *me* as a leader, or is this about *God* and *His* mission for our world? The question is not about how others see me (it is always possible to *project* a God agenda) but about my own personal priorities. Are they established by *my* ambition and goals, or is my ambition that of fulfilling *God's* purposes and goals? Without introspection on this question it is possible to be fooled about whose priorities we are looking after. Probably all of us have occasions or periods when we get our agendas confused with God's. And it is often when we have our priorities mixed up that we get ourselves into trouble.

This question of agendas and priorities becomes more significant as we grow in our leadership responsibility and scope. Responsibility brings with it power and authority. The temptation to act without considering God's agenda and priorities grows as our leadership scope and self-confidence grows. The more successful we are, the more critical it is to ensure that our motivations are centered on accomplishing God's agenda rather than our own.

We come to Christ as selfish, self-centered individuals who love our autonomy. Following Christ is a *process* in which we learn to do the will of the Father and to serve Christ rather than ourselves. That transformation takes place as we thoughtfully read His Word (His priorities are revealed there), learn to listen to His voice (as He speaks to our spirits), and spend time with Him in prayer (where we intentionally ask the Father what His priorities are for our lives and our ministries). In addition, we need to have a community of other leaders around us, through whom God often speaks to us. Intentional development of these relationships can be a significant check to our own sinful tendencies.

Anyone desiring transformation must daily confront the question of priorities. We must learn to live with sensitivity to God's Spirit. Spiritual transformation is always a cooperative effort between ourselves and the Holy Spirit. We must *want* to bring our lives into alignment with Him—and *take* the steps of obedience to do so. His Spirit then gives us the empowerment to carry out those choices to align with Him. We cannot do it on our own, but neither will the Holy Spirit do it for us. Paul was speaking of this cooperative effort when he wrote, "Since we live by the Spirit, let us keep in step with the Spirit" (Galatians 5:25).

Leaders are *culture makers* in that their attitudes and priorities become the culture of their organization as others take their cues from them. A highly ethical leader generally leads to a highly ethical culture. A results-oriented leader leads to a results-oriented culture. A disorganized leader often leads to a disorganized organization. Leaders define culture, good and bad, through the ongoing manifestation of their own priorities. Getting this right therefore takes on huge significance.

The ongoing growth and transformation of priorities to

match Christ's priorities becomes one of the leader's highest goals. It is impossible to separate the personal life of a leader from his or her leadership role. Who I am becomes a part of who the organization is, for better or for worse.

Transformation of Our Relationships

In many ways, the quality of our relationships is the best test of God's transformative work in our lives. As the apostle John wrote, "This is how we know what love is: Jesus Christ laid down his life for us. And we ought to lay down our lives for our brothers and sisters" (1 John 3:16). The same apostle in his Gospel records Jesus as saying, "I have given them the glory that you gave me, that they may be one as we are one—I in them and you in me—so that they may be brought to complete unity. Then the world will know that you sent me" (John 17:22-23). In other words, people will know we are Christians by our extraordinary and unselfish love for one another.

Transformation of our hearts is directly connected to the transformation of our relationships. A full understanding of God's grace in our lives becomes the ground for us to extend that grace to others on a regular basis, and it is grace that allows us to love, and love that transforms relationships. When I fully grasp how Christ loved me when I was unlovable, forgave me when I was at my worst, is patient with me when I don't deserve His patience, and continues to forgive me when I blow it—when I fully grasp the unconditional love of Christ to me—then I can extend that same love to others.

My ability to extend grace to others is directly connected to my understanding of the grace God has extended to me.

Transforming our relationships means learning to treat people as God treats us, seeing them as God sees us—as individuals made in His image and of infinite worth. In transformed relationships we want for others what God wants for them—that they reach their full potential—and we extend the same value and honor to others that God does to us. While the culture of the world says to use others for one's own benefit, Christ-followers see relationships as an extension of our relationship with Him, always wanting the best for others.

This is an especially critical issue for leaders who have authority over others and whose words, actions, and decisions impact others. Because good leaders have an agenda and are results-oriented, there is always the temptation to *use* people to achieve that agenda. Instead, leaders of deep influence work together with their people to develop a common mission, and together they achieve the mission through *serving* people and helping them flourish in the roles they play.

This is always a balancing act because leadership means that we must achieve results, resources are always in short supply, and getting the right people in the right seats on the bus is always a leadership challenge. Relational stewardship in leadership involves finding the right gifting for various positions, building healthy teams, and developing people into their God-given potential. Rather than *using* people, this is all about helping individuals become the men and women God designed them to be.

Leadership is about relational equity. We regularly make deposits to and withdrawals from that equity—withdrawals when we disempower or in some way break trust, and deposits when we treat people well and empower them. Thus transformation of our relationships is a key component, not only to the love we are called to live out, but to our leadership and the influence we exercise. Without healthy relationships, influence is deeply compromised.

TRANSFORMATION AS A LIFE PRIORITY

I would guess that most who read this chapter would whole-heartedly agree with what I have said. Agreement is not the challenge; it is finding the time to nurture our inner lives and allowing the Holy Spirit to transform us. As leaders, we don't get kudos for what is done behind the scenes, but the work of transformation is very much one that requires us to think, study, pray, be introspective, and work on our private lives even as we lead. Our schedules and busyness often get in the way of this important leadership work. Before we focus on others, we very much need to focus on ourselves and the work God desires to do in us. The greater the transformation, the deeper the influence we will have.

Wise leaders make their spiritual life and the Holy Spirit's intended transformation central. It is easy to focus on developing leadership strategies and strategic plans, building teams, and all the things leaders do. It's more difficult to stay close to

God, to evaluate our own lives against His, and to pay attention to the ongoing transformation of heart, thinking, priorities, and relationships. Yet these hidden areas of our lives are *the* most critical and central to being people of deep influence.

In our organization personal development is a high priority; we ask each individual to develop an annual plan for himself or herself. We think in terms of spiritual, relational, emotional, physical, and skill health. A reservoir of personal health will spill out in healthy leadership and relationships. All of us have met leaders whose spiritual, relational, and emotional health was problematic, and we know how the toxic effects hurt those around them.

Long ago I learned that formulas only work for some people. Usually not me. Spiritual transformation is a deeply personal business between the Holy Spirit and each of us. The Spirit gives us the insight and power to *take off* those things that displease Him and to *put on* those that reflect His character (see Ephesians 4:22-24).

I find three commitments common to those who enjoy deep influence: They *want* that transformative work, they *make* time in their busy lives to be with God and to reflect on their lives, and they actively *cooperate* with Him in areas where He speaks to them about needed change.

TRANSFORMATIONAL LEADERSHIP
The payoff for doing this kind of inner work is that transformed leaders are able to bring transformation to the ministries they lead. We sometimes overlook the fact that

organizations are often deeply in need of transformation and renewal, and it is the role of leaders to see to this need. Such is transformational leadership.

Transformational leadership in the Christian ministry arena is the deliberate creation of healthy, empowered, Spirit-led, collegial, effective ministries. It is the opposite of managing the status quo. The transformational leader sees his or her job as bringing transformation to all areas of the organization where malaise and bureaucracy have crept in, where spiritual sensitivity, empowerment, missional clarity, or focused results are lacking. Organizational renewal is never a onetime adjustment but always an ongoing concern.

At the individual level transformational leaders create a culture that encourages spiritual transformation; at the organizational level they create a culture where corporate spiritual vitality and missional clarity can flourish.

All good leaders are change agents, influencing organizations toward healthy structures, cultures, and ethos. Because organizations naturally tend to slide toward institutionalism and the comfortable, leaders must constantly ensure that they stay missional and focused. When a leader ceases to be transformational, he or she ceases to be effective.

One cannot take others where one has not been oneself. Transformational leadership starts with leaders who make transformation in their own lives a priority. Then they apply the same principles of spiritual, emotional, relational, and skill health to their team or organization.

There are far too many unhealthy work environments

today, even in the Christian arena. Often organizational illness reflects the leader who has not focused on his or her own transformation and has not brought transformation to his or her areas of responsibility. One of the greatest gifts a leader can give a staff is a life that is being constantly transformed by the Spirit, together with a commitment to bring the best possible transformation to the ministry.

WHEN TRANSFORMATION AND INFLUENCE MEET

Those who have made ongoing transformation of their lives a priority are magnets to others because they possess a unique set of character qualities that reflect the character of Christ. They are comfortable with God, and are therefore comfortable with themselves, because they understand grace and its implications. The grace they have experienced spills over into their relationships with others, as it did between Christ and those He met.

One is drawn to them because of the depth of their thinking. They are measured in their words, responses, and emotions. Their words—thoughtful, fair, full of grace, and often contrarian to the common wisdom of the day—evidence a mind that has been marinated in Scripture and in the wisdom of God.

They live differently from most. Behind their life choices are carefully thought-out priorities and commitments, which lead to an intentional rather than an accidental life. They are willing to say no to those things that God is not calling them to do. At the same time, they are often the first to help those in need, to extend grace to those who need it, to mentor and encourage others, and to make significant time for ministry in the midst of their schedules.

People love to be with them because they exude interest in others and are kind in their interactions, whether with a colleague or with a waitress in the local restaurant. They are gracious with those who disagree with them, patient with those who disappoint, forgiving of those who fail, and nonjudgmental in the gray areas of life. These are people we remember and adore.

That is who I want to be! And I know that I will only be such a man as I actively cooperate with the Holy Spirit, allowing Him to transform my character—my heart, thinking, priorities, and relationships—into that of Christ. It is then that I become the *me* He made *me* to be. It is then that I will have the deepest influence because it is the influence of Christ Himself—influence that comes from the core of who I am because my core is increasingly becoming like Jesus. The attraction of others to us becomes the attraction of others to Jesus through us.

For Reflection and Discussion

1. In your life, how is God currently working toward transformation of your heart, mind, priorities, and relationships?

2. What practices are regular parts of your life, which allow the Holy Spirit to bring transformation to you?

3. Of the four areas of transformation mentioned, on which do you need to focus in your life today?

4. What do you view as the connection between your own personal transformation and the ministry that you lead or participate in?

5. Are there areas in which your team or organization needs transformation? How can you influence that transformation?

CHAPTER FIVE

MANAGING THE SHADOW SIDE

I remember as a child making a game of trying to move fast enough to lose my shadow. It never worked. My shadow followed me no matter what I did. I could jump, dodge, and weave, and the shadow remained.

We all have a shadow side: It is the side of us that we like to forget and are reluctant to acknowledge. Because we neglect it, it often gets us into trouble with others and can severely compromise our influence, if not destroy it altogether. Deep influence is gained the hard way, as we have seen, and unfortunately it is easily lost. It can be compromised or destroyed quickly if we don't practice the discipline of managing our shadow side. The stronger our strengths, the longer our shadow!

This is not an easy chapter to read. It's no easier for me to write. As Christian leaders, each of us has an ideal *me* that we want to project to others—and that we believe about ourselves. We believe in spiritual transformation and desire that transformation for our lives. We are often disciplined to a fault in our effort to become all that God wants us to become. But as in my childhood game, we will never lose our shadow side until we finally meet Christ face to face. In the meantime, we need to understand ourselves well, know where the shadow side lies, and manage it carefully. We must allow the Holy Spirit to sensitize us to the darker facets of our wiring and areas of personal temptation.

In the book of Ephesians, Paul gives us examples of the shadow side: sensuality, deceitful desires, falsehood, stealing, unwholesome talk, grieving the Holy Spirit, bitterness, rage, anger, brawling, slander, malice, unforgiveness, impurity, greed, obscenity, foolish talk, course joking, and the list goes on (see 4:25–5:4). These behaviors are the residue of our lower nature, which has yet to be transformed into His likeness. Paul goes on to say, "For you were once darkness, but now you are light in the Lord. Live as children of light (for the fruit of the light consists in all goodness, righteousness and truth) and find out what pleases the Lord" (5:8-10).

It is easy to spot the shadow side in others—those behaviors that are unhealthy, that cause us frustration or anger. But none of us is special. Our issues may be different, but each of us has a shadow side that regularly threatens to lessen our influence and detract from the impact God desires us to have.

STRENGTHS AND LIABILITIES

Each strength we possess comes with a requisite downside—
a liability. When we exercise our strengths, we live in our
sweet spot, in the seat specially made for us, in the lane that
God created us for—*if* we are also managing the downsides
of those strengths.

Three of my five signature strengths according to
StrengthsFinder, a test developed by the Gallup Organization
to identify our unique strengths, are "maximizer," "strategic," and "achiever." As a maximizer, I want to always maximize ministry opportunity and leave nothing on the table.
This means that I will question the way we do things, and I
will always push for the most effective strategy to maximize
results with our people, resources, and opportunities. For me
as an organizational leader, this is a great strength to have,
and it has had a positive impact on the methodology of our
organization. As an achiever I want to accomplish the most
I can, which matches up with my type-A personality. The
strategic strength means that I am always looking for better
ways to do what we do.

But these strengths have their downsides as well. As a
maximizer, strategist, and achiever, I can easily become
impatient with strategies that merely add when they could
multiply. My impatience in itself is not always a problem,
but when it causes me to be less diplomatic, to respond
harshly, or in some way to devalue others who don't yet
"get it," my strengths have lost to their shadow side. I am
sure there are those who have viewed me over the years as

insensitive and uncaring in situations where I did not adequately manage the shadow side of these otherwise great signature strengths.

Knowing the shadow side of our strengths allows us to manage or compensate in ways that prevent the strengths from becoming liabilities. I have learned, when exercising my maximizer, strategic, and achiever strengths, to press more gently. I've learned that it's more effective to dialogue—not tell, much less command—in order to help others understand that multiplication is better than addition. And I have learned the hard way over the years that process and time are essential ingredients to moving people and organizations in a more effective direction.

I have a pastor friend who is the ultimate relationship guy. If he were to take the StrengthsFinder assessment, I am sure his number one strength would be "Woo," which means he influences others by bringing them into his orbit with the force of his friendly demeanor. He also has a gift for talking, as do most highly relational folks. Everyone in the church loves him because he is winsome and encouraging and people feel connected to him. He uses no manipulation; it's just who he is. Much of what he has accomplished as a leader in his church comes back to his winsome, relational style. It is a huge strength and I have watched it for years.

However, this great strength also has its liabilities— its shadow side. He has found over the years that, when dealing with some problems, he can "wing it" and get by with his relational skill rather than doing his homework on critical issues. That works for a while but not forever. Staff and leaders working for my friend often feel that they have been shortchanged by a lack of disciplined decision making. My friend has learned to do ministry by the seat of his pants rather than through team. He simply uses the force of his personality to convince others that his way is the right way.

And he is hard to disagree with. He is a debater who can dominate any conversation or any meeting—and usually does, sometimes leaving others feeling as though they cannot win and their opinions are not important. Because he is so likable, he often gets away with it, but not without cost. The cost is the disenfranchisement of others because they feel used, unheard, and devalued. His team meetings are not characterized by mutual dialogue but by his expounding. This has led to tension with his team and his board, who see only a one-man show. At one point my friend almost lost his church because of the shadow side of his relational strength.

Every strength brings with it a *liability*, a shadow side that, unless recognized and managed, will compromise the strength or even turn the strength into a greater negative than the strength was a positive. The latter case is the ultimate irony about our strengths. Misguided and unchecked, our strengths can become the very means of our loss of influence and effectiveness. It is on those shoals that many brilliant men and women of potentially great influence have shipwrecked!

"SPIRITUALITY" DOES NOT COMPENSATE FOR OUR SHADOW SIDE

Even a genuinely spiritual person can have difficulty recognizing his or her shadow side and dealing with it. The apostle Paul—a spiritual man if there ever was one—was a hard-driving, type-A, highly disciplined individual. When John Mark did not live up to his standards, Paul and Barnabas, two giants of the New Testament, came to such disagreement that they had to separate ways. So strong was the disagreement that Paul abandoned not only John Mark, but the very individual who had discipled and encouraged him when no one else would—Barnabas. The shadow side of his discipline and high standards (achiever?) alienated him from perhaps his best friend ever (see Acts 15:36-41).

Can you imagine the pain that Barnabas and John Mark felt when Paul took such a hard line? No amount of spirituality on Paul's part kept him from deeply hurting two individuals who loved him very much. Perhaps words like *arrogance* and *narcissism* and *impatience* found their way into Barnabas's mind as he processed his friendship and partnership gone wrong.

That Paul changed his mind about John Mark later in his life and requested his presence when he was in prison indicates to me that Paul had become more self-aware and was dealing with the downside of his driven personality. Paul was as deeply spiritual as any man who ever lived, and yet he too had a shadow side to his strengths—liabilities that hurt Barnabas and John Mark because he didn't recognize them at the time or failed to manage them well. He was probably well-meaning throughout, but he needed to learn to manage his shadow side.

There are also people who hide behind a gloss of "spirituality" to ignore or compensate for their shadow side. These are often Christian leaders who offer a spiritual explanation for even those difficulties caused by their own problems.

Dan is a leader who is black and white, always right, critical of others, and impervious to alternate points of view. He attracts followers like the Stepford wives, blindly following without thinking critically for themselves. Those who disagree with him are marginalized and devalued. But he always does this behind a facade of "spirituality" that no one can penetrate. When he is the only one in a group to take a certain position, he sees himself as a beleaguered prophet speaking truth to the blind. No amount of discussion or dialogue will shift him from his "correct" and "prophetic" point of view.

When his arrogant stubbornness causes problems in his organization, he interprets the conflict as spiritual warfare, and now those who disagree are unwitting "agents of Satan." His vocabulary is filled with unassailable spiritual references (how can you argue against God?) so that rational dialogue is hard or impossible and disagreements are doomed to end only one way.

Dan has caused huge pain for many people. Those who are smart enough to recognize his methodology stay away from him, leaving him with sycophants who become his blind disciples. Dan has spiritualized both his strengths and his liabilities in order to justify them, to avoid dealing with his shadow side, and to escape admission that his behaviors often hurt others.

In essence his method for dealing with his shadow side is narcissism hidden behind a Christian vocabulary that keeps him from accepting accountability for his shadow side. Because of the spiritual facade, many are afraid to name his conduct for what it is—self-centered, hurtful to others, and frankly emotionally sick. Meanwhile, Dan continues on in purported bliss, in denial about his shadow side, leaving a trail of wounded people in his wake.

PROFESSIONAL CRITIC

Another methodology for avoiding accountability for our shadow side is to become a professional critic of others. Every leader has encountered these folks at one time or another. They are quick to criticize and distrust. They frequently question the motives of others, without doing their homework to validate their skepticism. They love to become enmeshed with other critics—the best way to verify their version of reality. And yes, there are plenty of these in the church and in Christian organizations. They twist motives, conversations, or actions to match their view of reality, which is often skewed.

What is really going on behind the professional critic's behavior is often the justification of his or her own behavior. Focusing on the critical assessment of others helps avoid critical assessment of one's own shadow side. Often the glue that holds professional critics' friendships together is not a common mission but a common enemy—someone "out there," on whom they can focus their unhappiness, anger, or unresolved personal issues—often a leader, because leaders are most visible.

These unhealthy individuals accumulate pockets of unhealthy individuals who all speak the same "language." These foster unhealthy organizations through their closed circles of opinions and criticisms.

THE RIGHTEOUS STRUGGLE

There are many ways of coping with one's own shadow side. One is to face it and seek to deal with it; make no mistake, this is a lifelong endeavor. Others are to mask it, to ignore it, to spiritualize it, or to focus on the shadow side of others rather than on one's own.

People of deep influence never mask or ignore. We realize that we are people who have a lower nature and that the process of spiritual transformation means exegeting ourselves so that we bring every aspect of our lives—especially the shadow side—under the lordship of Christ.

Often we resist dealing forthrightly with our shadow side because we are ashamed that we even struggle with one. This shame is mistaken; it is a misunderstanding of God's work in our lives. Every one of us is a work in progress. Every one of us lives with the liabilities of being human, and we are therefore imperfect and limited in our understanding of ourselves and of others. Paul understood this when he said in Philippians 3:16, "Let us live up to what we have already attained." God does not expect perfection but simply obedience to all He has shown us at this point in our lives.

Furthermore, humble individuals are transparent about both their strengths and their weaknesses, their areas of victory and their liabilities. Those who pretend they have it all together fool themselves but not those around them. Our influence is not gained by pretending to be something we are not but by being transparent in our walk with God. People of deep influence don't hide who they are or the struggles they have. In fact, it is precisely because they are honest about their struggles that we can identify with them; it is their commitment to live with authenticity that draws us to them.

MANAGING OUR STRENGTHS' LIABILITIES

Because many individuals have not understood that their strengths can also be their greatest liabilities, they simply don't pay appropriate attention to the downside of their strengths. However, people of deep influence are acutely aware of both their strengths and the liabilities associated with those strengths. And they pay at least as much attention to the liabilities.

Think about this: Our strengths are just that—strengths. Over time, if we are living in our sweet spot, they grow and develop without a whole lot of attention from us. They come to us naturally. I have the natural ability to think strategically.

I can envision future potential in five or ten years without even thinking about it. What is hard or impossible for others is second nature for me. The liabilities that come with that particular gift, however, are not as obvious to me—for example, impatience with those who don't see what I can see, or the potential that others may see my confidence as arrogance.

I will never forget a meeting I had years ago with a bright young woman who reported to me. She came into my office to share an idea that she thought had great potential. About two minutes into our conversation her eyes flashed with anger and she said, "Don't ever look that way at me again!"

I said, "What do you mean? What way?"

She said, "I can tell from your eyes that you have already dismissed my idea as one that won't work!"

She was right. My eyes had given me away; I was sure that her idea would not work. My strategic strength had become my liability by sending her a message of disempowerment. I apologized and learned from the experience.

Our strengths come naturally. The corresponding liabilities are not obvious to us unless we spend significant time understanding them and the ways they can hurt people if not managed.

People do not achieve deep influence by focusing on the deficits of others but by attending first to their own deficits. They are deeply self-aware, and they think carefully about their own motivations and how they treat others. They have developed an inner early warning system that alerts them when they are veering toward the shadow side, and they discipline themselves to manage their liabilities. They understand the counsel of Christ: that we are first responsible for taking the plank out of our own eye before we try to take the speck out of someone else's eye (see Matthew 7:3-5).

All of us have areas of our lives where we are blind to the ways our actions impact others. A large part of managing our shadow side is understanding not only how we perceive ourselves but how others perceive us and why. Because we are dealing with blind spots, the only way we can achieve this awareness is by receiving feedback from others. And that requires self-confidence, humility, and a nothing-to-prove-nothing-to-lose attitude. Many young leaders resist such feedback; it is threatening and uncomfortable. I know; I have been there!

A valuable lesson I have learned over the years is to welcome and not resist feedback—particularly from those who love me and have my best interests in mind. My wife, Mary Ann, is one of those who will always tell me the truth, and I know she does it out of love and concern. I have a trusted group of colleagues and friends who have the same right to speak into my life and whose counsel I trust. I've also recruited a prayer team who regularly share with me feedback that they have discerned as they have interceded on my behalf. I would rather know where I have blind spots or am being misperceived than live like the emperor with no clothes, oblivious to his nakedness. The key, of course, is knowing whom one can trust to have one's best interests in mind.

I have learned to proactively ask for feedback from those I trust, rather than just hope it will come. I know, for instance, that I can be perceived as distant by some, even when I'm not feeling that way. I would not know this without feedback. Knowing that such a perception is possible, I can work to find ways to connect with those who might otherwise see me as distant.

I have learned, for instance, that the more candid I am about myself and my struggles, the more approachable I become. This has led me to be far more self-disclosing with those around me than I was as a young leader, when I thought that such self-disclosure would be seen as weakness. While I may not be wired like some who are deeply relational, I'm able to connect deeply with others through authentic self-disclosure.

The more we learn about ourselves—both through our own awareness and from those around us—the better we become at playing to our strengths and minimizing our liabilities. There are many things I wish I had known about myself years ago. I am thankful that I know them now. And I want to continue in my quest for healthy self-awareness for the sake of the influence that I hope to have in the future.

COUNSEL, TIME, AND PRAYER

Leaders who build healthy teams of highly competent individuals use those teams to help alleviate their own liabilities. Even though I have a strong sense of direction and a great deal of experience in dealing with complex organizational issues, I know that counsel from wise individuals is far better than dealing with the issue by myself.

I am convinced that the wisdom of others often prevents our liabilities and our limited perspective from compromising our decisions. When faced with a difficult situation, I *never* respond without significant dialogue with trusted colleagues. They have prevented me from making stupid calls in any number of instances. There is simply too much at stake for me to make unilateral decisions in tough spots. And it is often hard to separate our own emotions from what is best organizationally, especially when we are the subject of the conversation!

Bringing trusted colleagues into hard situations is also a check against any tendency to lead autocratically or to deal with problematic personnel in unfair or harsh ways. Even as a senior leader, I have accountability in my leadership and make decisions through the involvement of other senior leaders. Again, this becomes a check against human tendencies to lead out of personal preferences, pride, or the limited perspective any one of us has by ourselves.

Another hedge against our troublesome shadow side is to resist the temptation to respond quickly. Quick decisions often come out of emotion, and emotion is often influenced more by our shadow side than by wisdom. Difficult decisions and difficult people frequently stir anxiety in us. The anxiety makes us feel as if we need to do something *now*, when in reality waiting, thinking, and getting counsel is often far wiser. A wise, reasoned, unemotional response takes time.

How many of us have sent an emotional e-mail in the heat of the moment, unfiltered by wisdom, that we wish we could rescind? Even if we have reason to be angry, in anger we are likely to contribute further to the problem.

Time is our ally in most difficult decisions. I have committed to a practice of refraining from action before I have agreement with one or more trusted colleagues that the time is right and the approach is wise. The knottier the problem, the longer I will usually wait, unless there is an overwhelming reason to act quickly.

The wisdom of the Holy Spirit is critical to keeping our shadow side from compromising our leadership. One of the reasons that time is an ally in hard decisions is that it gives us time to pray, to think, and to allow the Holy Spirit to give us a perspective that transcends human understanding. I am constantly amazed at the way solutions come to mind as I think, pray, dialogue with colleagues, and allow God time.

One of the traps that good leaders fall into is to start to believe that, because they have had leadership success, they are always capable of making the right decisions. Our very success can lead to decisions that are unwise when we trust our own leadership instincts and choose not to seek counsel or take the time for prayer and evaluation. The more success we enjoy as leaders, the more careful we ought to be not to believe our own press, to remain humble, to seek wise counsel, and to take the time for prayerful consideration. Success can lead either to greater leadership wisdom or to the hubristic shadow side.

COMMON VULNERABILITIES

Some vulnerabilities are not as obvious as others. Sometimes the very things we yearn for can become our greatest vulnerability! This is true of success. All of us want our ministries and organizations to be successful and to impact as many as possible. But with success come major liabilities: pride, self-confidence that can push out our need for God or others, and a feeling that somehow we are immune to temptation. After all, have we not successfully negotiated life and ministry to get to where we are?

It is not wrong to seek success, but we must recognize that the greater our success, the more vulnerable we are to its shadow side. One of the classic signs of the shadow side of success is lack of accountability. Following a twisted logic, successful individuals can come to the conclusion that they do not need the counsel and accountability of others—probably the very things that got them where they are. As they move away from accountability and toward risky autonomy, they listen to fewer and fewer people and often marginalize those who disagree with their perspective. Pride is one of the most insidious aspects of our shadow side, for it elevates us above others and sometimes above God. Pride, autonomy, lack of accountability, and eventually twisted thinking come in a package often fueled by success.

With success comes the tendency of others to curry favor rather than to speak honestly. It isolates because of the increased demands that success exacts. Those increased demands lessen time for thinking, self-reflection, and close relationships, which are so foundational for spiritual transformation, self-knowledge, and intimacy with Christ.

Successful men and women go in one of two directions—toward humility and accountability or toward pride and autonomy. The former deepens influence while the latter will eventually cause influence to dissipate.

We are also vulnerable in times of failure. This is particularly true for individuals in ministry whose identity is wrapped up with what they do—confusing their identity in Christ with a ministry identity. Failure calls into question our calling, our competency, God's intervention, and sometimes our very faith.

In times of failure we have two options. Either we press into God in a new way, choosing faith and optimism, or we settle for bitterness and a diminished life, perhaps holding God responsible for our situation. Each of us is responsible for the direction he or she chooses. Life comes undone for all of us at one time or another. These difficult times present either an opportunity to build character and experience, or a pit in which we sink and wallow.

We have seen how suffering is a prerequisite to deep influence. Failure is one form of suffering. How we respond will determine its positive or negative impact on our lives. I came close to throwing in the ministry towel after my difficult pastorate. How grateful I am today that I walked away from that brink! I now see that failure as one of God's most effective tools in my shaping.

Between success and failure are periods of life that just are.

And sometimes—as when David sat in his palace while his troops were out at war—boredom sets in and our restlessness makes us vulnerable to temptation, to laziness, to moving away from intimacy with God. Periods of restlessness, when boredom sets in, are actually wonderful opportunities for growth because at such times we usually have extra time on our hands, time to do something productive that will build into our future influence.

Intellectual laziness is one of the most acute issues facing those in ministry, especially in their forties and fifties. The world keeps changing and morphing, and unless we continue to grow and lead in our spheres of influence, we become superfluous, just as so many middle and senior managers in business have become.

The apostle Paul understood this risk and would have nothing of it in his own life: "Forgetting what is behind and straining toward what is ahead, I press on toward the goal to win the prize for which God has called me heavenward in Christ Jesus" (Philippians 3:13-14). Each of us has a prize to strive toward unceasingly—fulfilling God's call on our lives. To settle for anything but the complete fulfillment of that call is to settle for less than God intends for us.

INDIVIDUAL VULNERABILITIES

All of us have unique vulnerabilities—places or times or situations where the shadow side can show up if we do not carefully plan to remain self-aware and compensate for them. Vulnerabilities are not something to be ashamed of—we are human—but to be aware of and to manage so that the vulnerabilities do not turn into something worse.

I know that I am vulnerable when I am overly tired. So does my family, who can receive the brunt of my cranky attitude. I also know that I am prone to periods of depression if I do not get enough rest. At the same time I tend to say yes to too many opportunities, and it takes people around me to help me moderate my schedule and think realistically about what my body can handle.

The Evil One is described as a prowling lion waiting to devour (see 1 Peter 5:8, HCSB). Lions love the tall grass where they can hide, watching for just the right moment to attack. They watch for the laggard of the herd, the vulnerable animal, and then at the right moment they launch the attack—often fatally. That is an accurate description of the Evil One, who loves to discourage, hurt, or take down God's people. It is also why we must be even more aware in our times of vulnerability than in our times of strength.

This again takes us back to the importance of self-knowledge, acute awareness of our strengths and weaknesses. Satan wants us to live unexamined lives, while the Father wants us to be astutely aware and wise in how we live. After all, every day there is a lion on the prowl, waiting for a moment when he can launch an attack.

Because I am by nature an introvert (in an extrovert's job), my tendency would be to go off by myself when I am tired and worn out. But that is when I am personally most vulnerable, so I compensate by spending time *with* family or friends. Knowing my vulnerable moments, I go on the offensive in order to stay healthy.

I don't need to repeat the list of temptations, common to man, that assail us in our weak moments. The list is long, and apart from the empowerment of the Holy Spirit we are weak. You know what your vulnerabilities are, and I know mine. The question is whether we are intentional in our awareness and whether we have a plan to offset those temptations so that vulnerabilities do not lead to casualties.

ANTIDOTES TO THE SHADOW SIDE

There is no escaping our shadow side, but there are ways to minimize its damage in our lives and in the lives of others. I believe that there are six major antidotes to our shadow sides. None of them is enough in itself, but practiced together they are powerful tools that lead to deep influence. They really involve choices, so I am going to posit them as choices we make. And each of us makes them regularly.

Living in Isolation or Living in Relationship

We live in a highly individualistic culture, at least in the West. It is easy for us to live in isolation rather than in relationship. Yet it is in authentic relationships with others that life rubs on life, where iron sharpens iron, where we are challenged to be our best and to become all that God intends us to be (see Proverbs 27:17). Mary Ann and I have made the cultivation of key relationships (we call them friends for life) a high priority in our lives. I am convinced that the healthier our relationships, the healthier we are. The more isolated we live, the greater the opportunity for the shadow side to show itself—and ultimately to hurt our influence.

Living with Autonomy or Living with Accountability

This follows from the first choice. Choosing to live in authentic relationship is a choice to live with accountability rather than with autonomy because with relationship comes healthy accountability. If I were to choose to do something stupid with my life, I know a good number of friends who would show up at my door and call me to reason.

These are people I trust, whose feedback I value and who I know have my best interests in mind. Choosing to live with accountability is a major hedge against our shadow sides becoming liabilities. Those who live without accountability and whose relationships are only with those who affirm them almost always end up on the shoals.

Living with Self-Knowledge or Living an Unexamined Life

There are things I don't like about me! But knowing those things is far better than ignoring them and pretending they don't exist. The better I know me, the better the chance I have that I can cooperate with God so that I become the me I want to be, the me He made me to be. That means knowing how God wired me, where my shadow side is, what my unique vulnerabilities are, and where and how I can hurt others because of my makeup.

People of deep influence are self-aware and appropriately introspective, so that they understand their motivations, their tendencies, areas where they are vulnerable to temptation, and how they deal with those vulnerabilities. Their self-knowledge includes an understanding of God's amazing grace in their lives. They are not overwhelmed by their sin, but by God's grace; they are not seeking to prove themselves to God, but simply to live in His presence, forgiveness, and grace on a daily basis.

Living with Humility or Living with Pride

If we are living with self-knowledge, it is very hard to be prideful. We know that we are justified by Christ (declared not guilty, cleansed) and that He is sanctifying us (making us more and more like Him) as we walk with Him, but we also know that we live with brokenness and sin and shadow sides that we wish were not there. Humility is recognizing that life is about Him, not us, and that everything good in us is because of Him and His work in our lives.

Pride is a rejection of God's place in our lives and an elevation of ourselves. A rather presumptuous attitude! Pride in me does not want to know the truth about myself and actually promotes an alternate truth about who I really am. Humility has a nothing-to-prove-nothing-to-lose attitude that is not afraid to acknowledge the true me, does not need to wear a facade to pretend there is an alternate me, and realizes that I am completely indebted to God for anything good.

Living Intentionally or Living Accidentally

We are most vulnerable to shadow sides when we live without a plan, without the discipline of carefully chosen priorities lived out in a purposeful fashion. Careless living allows our shadow sides to show up without our even being aware of it.

I have never met an individual of deep influence who lived carelessly. The framework that helps such a person minimize the impact of his or her shadow side is one of careful thought and intentional practice. Managing our shadow side necessarily requires a plan that comes out of deep self-knowledge.

Living in Intimacy with Christ
or Living in Distance from Christ

Our connection to Christ is a critical element in managing our shadow side. In intimacy with Him, we allow His Holy Spirit to reveal Himself to us and to peel back layers of our lives to reveal sin and areas where He wants to work. Certainly the closer we stay to Christ, the more receptive we are to His nudging in our lives. The further we are from Him, the more we rely on self for our understanding and wisdom—a dangerous practice.

As the writer of the book of Hebrews put it,

> The word of God is alive and active. Sharper than
> any double-edged sword, it penetrates even to
> dividing soul and spirit, joints and marrow; it judges
> the thoughts and attitudes of the heart. Nothing in

all creation is hidden from God's sight. Everything
is uncovered and laid bare before the eyes of him to
whom we must give account.
HEBREWS 4:12-13

When we allow the Scriptures to be a mirror in which we
see our lives, and when we allow the Holy Spirit to speak to
us about our lives, we will become sensitized to our shadow
side and allow God to manifest His character even in those
difficult areas.

DON'T IGNORE THE SHADOW SIDE

Our dislike for our shadow side makes it easy to ignore,
but pretending it is not there is not an option for people of
deep influence. It is easy to look out the window at others,
but much harder to look in the mirror at ourselves. Wise
individuals spend far more time looking in the mirror than
out the window. They know that understanding their own
inner dynamics is foundational to fulfilling God's potential
for them. They never ignore their shadow side!

For Reflection and Discussion

1. How would you describe the strengths God has given
   you? What are the shadow sides of those strengths?

2. Which aspects of your shadow side—in life and in
   leadership—are most likely to negatively impact you and
   those around you? In other words, can you identify your
   unique vulnerabilities?

3. Do you pay enough attention to these aspects of your life? If not, which steps of self-examination will you take next?

4. What strategies do you use to manage your shadow side? Of the "antidotes" we examined, which do you excel at and which need more attention?

5. Who are the people in your life who give you regular feedback regarding your shadow side? If you have no one, whom will you invite and how?

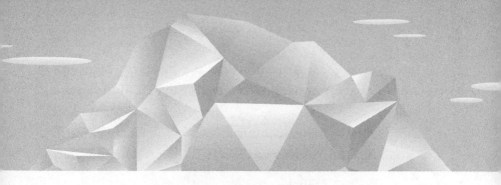

CHAPTER SIX

EMOTIONAL INTELLIGENCE (EQ)

Pastor Jeff has a history of unresolved issues with leaders at various levels in his church. Deeply needing affirmation, when he is challenged or perceives that people disagree with him, he marginalizes them—often by neglecting them. Through his lenses people are either with him or against him, and those who are "against" him he writes off. As a result he has effectively divided his own board into "supporters" and "detractors." In addition, his staff know there are issues they cannot discuss with him without risking being marginalized and even driven from the church, as has happened to some.

Because of his defensiveness and insecurity, Jeff has left a trail of emotionally wounded volunteers, former leaders, and staff in his wake. Many have quietly gravitated out of the church. Yet in Jeff's view the fault in each case was not his, but the other's. He is unable to negotiate conflict; nor does he know how to apologize in a way that heals the relationships he has shattered. And his hunger for emotional buttressing from others is insatiable.

Jeff's issues illustrate the importance of *emotional intelligence* in leadership. In fact, few factors are more significant in leadership than emotional intelligence, often labeled EQ. High EQ on the part of the leader creates a healthy culture for the whole organization. On the other hand, low EQ creates an equally unhealthy culture; it is the nemesis of many leaders—and, unfortunately, of those they lead. Jeff's low EQ has been the cause of pain and chaos in his church. Your EQ matters. A lot.

People of deep influence are people who do all they can to maintain and enhance their emotional intelligence. Low emotional intelligence can severely limit our influence because low EQ gets in the way of healthy relationships.

It is critical to understand the connection between the EQ of a leader and the culture of the organization he or she leads. This is easily seen in congregations where gracious leaders create a gracious culture, whereas black-and-white leaders create just the opposite. Leaders who cannot negotiate conflict in a healthy way create organizations with the same deficit.

Consider these other warning signs of low emotional intelligence.

- When challenged I am defensive.
- I display a lack of empathy or understanding, leaving people feeling hurt.
- I can be narcissistic ("it's all about me").
- I need to get my own way.
- I control others, rather than empower them.
- I use spiritual terms like "God told me" or "spiritual warfare" to shut down discussion.
- I have a lack of flexibility to negotiate a win-win solution.
- I hold grudges and don't forgive easily.
- I don't play on a team well.
- I have a lack of sensitivity to how actions or words affect others.
- I have an inability to state my position clearly while maintaining good relationships with those who disagree with me.
- I can display cynicism and mistrust toward others.
- I have a poor understanding of my strengths and weaknesses.
- I can have a victim mentality ("I'm the victim, conflict is always the other's fault").
- I have a black-and-white view of the world ("good guys, bad guys, little between"), leading to demonization of others.
- I need to be popular.
- I easily become enmeshed in other people's issues.
- I have high personal anxiety over aspects of my job.

- I often say one thing to one individual and another thing to others.

Do you see any of these signs of low EQ in yourself? Those who don't face their own truth are destined to short-circuit their own growth and effectiveness. In addition to examining yourself before God, consider asking your spouse and a trusted colleague to read this chapter and to note any positive or negative EQ characteristics they see in you. All of us have some areas of problematic EQ that can get us into trouble at predictable times.

Leadership ability hinges just as much on one's emotional health as it does on one's spiritual health. A large number of ministry relationship problems are related to the EQ of the leader or of others in the ministry.

Emotional intelligence is the ability to understand ourselves, to know what drives us, to accurately understand how we are perceived by others, to understand how we relate to others, and to control our emotions in healthy ways. EQ measures whether we have the relational skills to work synergistically with others while holding a personal position on a matter and whether we allow others to speak into our lives or our work without defensiveness. Healthy relationships require high EQ, and leadership is all about relationships and people. One can lead from a position of authority with low EQ, but one cannot lead through deep influence without healthy EQ.

I believe that we pay far too little attention to emotional

issues in the hiring of leaders, in the building of teams, and in our own lives. Many brilliant individuals with low emotional intelligence leave havoc in their wakes. Let's examine several key issues related to the leader's EQ.

INSECURITY OR SECURITY

Many symptoms of low emotional intelligence stem from basic insecurities on the part of a leader. Jeff's insecurities come from a deep fear of failure. Because he fears failure, he cannot afford to be wrong, which leads to defensive behaviors, making it hard for people to tell him how they see things or for him to resolve conflict. In addition, his own fear of failure overflows to his staff, who receive the loud message that "everything has to be perfect," leaving them constantly trying to meet his unreasonable expectations.

Insecure leaders are responsible for much leadership dysfunction, while personal security—being comfortable with who we are and how God made us—is the foundation for healthy leadership. When we lead out of personal insecurity, our own issues cloud our leadership and spill over on others.

The symptoms of insecurity are many: defensive attitudes, a need to be right, a desire for control, anger when things don't go our way, marginalization of those who don't agree with us, a spirit of criticism, a felt need to be liked rather than respected, and an inability to differ with others while staying connected.

Most people want to be liked, but a leader's desire to be liked often hurts his or her leadership. Leaders often default to being one of the boys (or girls) in their desire to be accepted, when in fact leadership requires them to maintain a certain degree of social distance. Good leaders desire collegial relationships but manage also to retain their leadership ability. When leaders default to being just one of the team, they are unlikely to press into core issues that would cause friction in their friendships. Ironically, while they might enjoy being friends with us, those we lead are more interested in the security of a leader who is setting the course and holding the tiller.

As I look back over my young leadership days, I can see many instances when my "need" to be right stemmed from my own basic insecurity as a leader. One of the great gifts of time for healthy leaders is that they learn to become comfortable in their own skin, with their particular God-given strengths and weaknesses. They adopt a nothing-to-prove-nothing-to-lose attitude.

Getting to healthy security and eliminating insecurity is a lifelong process for all of us. Developing an acute awareness of the ways our insecurity manifests itself can help us modify our behavior. Giving a few trusted others in our lives permission to reflect back honest feedback in these areas is not only helpful but demonstrates good EQ.

DEFENSIVENESS OR OPENNESS

Defensive leaders hurt themselves because their defensiveness prevents people from telling them the truth; and it's difficult to lead people whose view of the leader goes unshared and unknown. I would rather know about thoughts and perceptions I don't like, than not know.

The root of defensiveness is usually personal insecurity. The logic goes something like this: "If I am wrong, then I am not a good leader, so I cannot afford to be wrong. If I cannot afford to be wrong, I will push back against those who think their ideas are better." Ironically, in adopting a defensive posture, leaders actually lose credibility with others, even though they feel they have preserved it by defending their position. Defensive leaders live with the *illusion* that they know what people think, when in reality their defensiveness leaves them clueless and deeply vulnerable.

The cost of defensiveness is not only ignorance of what others think, but also a loss of intellectual capital. It is by means of multiple counselors and robust dialogue that we come to the best decisions and build a shared ownership of the team's strategy. But this requires the ability to engage in honest and forthright dialogue. An insecure and defensive leader stifles such dialogue.

Over the years I have adopted a principle that I seek to live by: an attitude of nothing-to-prove nothing-to-lose. If I have nothing to prove, I no longer need to be right. If I have nothing to prove, then by definition I have nothing to lose.

Equipped with an attitude of nothing-to-prove nothing-to-lose, I remind myself that it is okay when others push back or even attack (it happens to all leaders). I no longer need to be right, nor do I fear being proved wrong (all of us are wrong sometimes). I can just be me, with calm openness to the opinions of others. I can listen and even disagree without defensiveness. In fact, it is through nondefensive receptiveness that I get the very best thoughts from my team and from the organization I lead.

Healthy leaders work constantly on developing an open, rather than defensive, persona. They do this by first controlling the natural tendency toward defensive reactions when others disagree with or criticize their position. Rather than going defensive, they ask questions and make reflecting statements like, "If I hear you right, you are saying . . ." or "Unpack that for me so that I better understand what you are saying."

In doing so, they are giving the other person permission to speak into an issue rather than battle a defensive reaction that shuts down the conversation. Staying engaged conveys an implicit message: "I am willing to hear and to talk," while defensive words or facial expressions say, "The discussion is over."

Healthy leaders choose to put aside their own personal insecurities for the sake of organizational and missional health. They understand that the debates and deliberations are not about them personally but about the work to which God has called them. So they are willing to put up with a degree of discomfort for the sake of a healthy organization.

CONTROL OR EMPOWERMENT

Another component of low emotional intelligence is a dysfunctional desire to control, which pervades many teams and organizations. Insecure leaders feel a need to control others, while secure leaders set boundaries within which they release staff to use their gifts and wiring to accomplish the task. If we are afraid to fail, we will not take the risk that our staff might do something substandard or might cause us to look bad. Thus, in our insecurity, we feel threatened by good people, and we try to control others and tell them what to do. It is really *our* personal insecurity that causes us to distrust others, their gifts, and their ability to get the job done.

In contrast, empowerment of others comes from an attitude that our mission is about *us* rather than *me*. My role as a leader is not to call all the plays but to find and deploy good people, working in the synergy of a team to accomplish our mission.

I am convinced that control is the natural tendency in every society and is a direct result of the Fall. It is very interesting to study the example of Christ with His disciples. He led through influence, not control. In fact, after His resurrection He handed over His most precious possession—the church—to the apostles to lead. He was willing to trust them and the Holy Spirit working through them.

This empowering culture was then passed on by Paul in Ephesians 4:11-12, where he wrote that leaders in the church were "to equip [God's] people for works of service"—to give ministry responsibility away. Those who feel a need to control don't trust others, which reflects either the kinds of people they have hired or their own low emotional intelligence. The inability to release good people is actually a sign of pride because the underlying assumption is that "no one can do it as well as *I* can." Good team members will not long work for leaders who cannot release them to use their gifts and abilities to maximum advantage. Those who empower and release have far deeper influence than those who control and micromanage.

NARCISSISM OR HUMILITY

Insecurity is also at the root of narcissism. This is by far the most difficult emotional-intelligence problem to deal with among leaders, and many leaders suffer from it. For narcissists, the world revolves around them, they are always right, they don't listen to others, and they take the credit for what is accomplished. They are almost impossible to talk to about their condition, and they usually will not see it.

Narcissists don't like accountability and generally surround themselves with staff or board members whom they can manipulate and control. When confronted, they fight back hard, sometimes with anger, other times with debate and manipulation. They intend to win, whatever it takes. In ministry, narcissists often hide behind a spiritual facade and "God's direction or will." They are stubbornly unapproachable and divide people into two camps—those who are for them and those who are against them.

Because organizations are impacted by the EQ of the leader, those led by narcissists are usually dysfunctional. Since narcissists don't navigate conflict in a healthy manner, the organization often also fails in this respect. That is why narcissistic pastors often split the churches they lead. They never see conflict as their fault, so it is very difficult to resolve. In fact, almost all conflict is seen in light of "good and evil" or "spiritual warfare," which paints a picture that is difficult to refute. They create a culture that is difficult to change for years to come.

I am sometimes asked by staff members what to do if they work for a narcissistic leader. Generally I suggest they leave. They will not be able to help that leader see who he or she really is, and they will likely be hurt along the way, often deeply. The organization is likely to experience great pain because of its leader's low EQ. The only hope is a board that is willing to confront and fire a narcissistic leader, if necessary. But this happens only rarely because this kind of leader works hard to gather people he or she can control. Most others end up leaving for healthier pastures.

ENMESHMENT OR SELF-DEFINITION

A common issue related to low emotional intelligence is relational enmeshment. This happens when we allow ourselves to identify so closely with someone else that we take on his or her issue or offense as our own. This happens in families all the time: Two members of the family triangulate against a third, rather than dealing with problems directly. Tom has a conflict with Mary and talks to Sam about Mary. Sam takes up Tom's offense and gangs up with Tom to pressure Mary into conformity. Sam has become enmeshed with Tom.

This happens in churches and workplaces frequently. It is a violation of Matthew 18:15; it's the coward's way out of dealing with conflict. Rather than directly addressing the person with whom we have the conflict, we bring someone else into the equation and enmesh him or her in the problem. Rather than leading through deep influence, we are essentially using manipulation to get our way. This is not a fair way to compete in the world of ideas because healthy individuals will not respond in kind. And it inevitably divides people rather than unifying them.

Healthy individuals do not allow themselves to be drawn into other people's conflicts, nor do they draw others into theirs. They may well seek to help other individuals solve their problems in a healthy manner, but they do not take on the offenses of others.

Often, unhealthy leaders triangulate or enmesh others in their issues by playing the victim role. They communicate their hurt to those who are sympathetic and draw those folks into their circle of pain, setting them against those whom they perceive to have wronged them. It is dangerous and harmful when pastors do this, because those they enmesh have no way of solving the issue since they are not a part of the dispute. So even when pastors resolve their original conflict, those they have enmeshed often continue to carry ill will toward the "offending" party.

I have watched pastors divide their boards by choosing to triangulate with sympathetic board members against "the enemies." I have also seen unhealthy board members do the same thing. Long after the original problem is resolved, the board remains divided.

In contrast, a key component of high EQ is the ability

to be "self-defined." Self-defined individuals are comfortable with who they are. They can clearly articulate their own positions in a way that does not force others to agree and does not demonize those who disagree. They can say, "This is what I think, and why. Now tell me how you see it." In doing this, leaders make their position clear, along with their rationale, *and* open the door for honest conversation that can hopefully lead to a shared understanding.

A healthily self-defined leader can conduct dialogue even with those who strenuously disagree with him or her. Jeff can state his position but *cannot* stay connected relationally with those who disagree. Thus the conversation ends without any resolution. The ability to defend a position and stay connected with others who disagree is a key component to healthy relationships. It is usually in ongoing dialogue that one comes to mutually acceptable conclusions, as long as we are dealing with people who also have a high level of emotional health. Discussions with those of low EQ often go nowhere. Thus our ability to discern the EQ of others becomes a factor in how we deal with them.

Self-definition requires leaders to think well before they state a position, then also to open the door for nondefensive dialogue. If staff members know that they can honestly push back without repercussions and know that they will also be heard, it is often possible to come to a more refined position that works for everyone.

Self-definition is a powerful leadership tool because it clarifies the leader's values, convictions, attitudes, and actions. The more consistent these are, the more security is sensed by those who work for him or her. Followers know what to expect, they know the leader's convictions and guiding principles, and they don't fear irrational change or unhealthy triangulation.

ANGER OR PERSONAL CONTROL

There is no more destructive tendency among leaders than a short temper. Quick anger is a sign of an unhealthy individual who is struggling with internal issues, which erupt in unhealthy ways and hurt self and others. Anger causes us to say things that cannot be taken back and to make decisions that lack wisdom and discernment. Numerous times in the Scriptures we are exhorted to get rid of our anger and replace it with patience, perseverance, love, self-control, and wise responses (see Colossians 3:1-17; Ephesians 4:25-5:2). Anger is a symptom of low emotional intelligence and spiritual immaturity, while self-control is a sign of health.

I am saddened at how often people rupture relationships with others because they have made knee-jerk assumptions—often deeply faulty—about motives or actions and become angry. In the process, people are hurt, God's reputation is compromised, His mission is thwarted, and ultimately the Evil One wins. How we respond to his relational meddling and manipulation is our choice.

Rather than responding in anger, healthy individuals ask key questions. First, do I have my facts right? Wise individuals know that secondhand information is often faulty. They also know that there are two or more sides to every story.

Before we draw our own conclusions, we ought to consider the real possibility that there is more to the situation than we know, then either hold our own counsel or verify the information before drawing conclusions.

Second, is there another explanation for what I have heard or observed? Over the years I have discovered that most of the time, when I have chosen to draw negative conclusions about a person or situation, I learn that my initial assumptions were not correct. Each time I am stung by the realization of how quickly we can jump to the wrong conclusions.

Third, have I talked to the individual myself to attempt resolution? It is amazing how honest conversation and questions can restore what otherwise would have been left on the scrap heap of severed relationships. It is often helpful to involve a neutral, third party to help those in conflict hear one another and to clarify assumptions, actions, and possible solutions.

Fourth, have I contributed in any way to the failure of the relationship? Often we choose not to resolve issues because it means that we ourselves must admit that we bear responsibility. It is far easier in the short run to save face and paint the picture that we have been aggrieved than to admit to ourselves and others that we also have been wrong. Such an admission takes humility and honesty.

Where anger is prevalent, it is crucial to get help to determine its source. It will destroy otherwise good leadership. Leaders of deep influence foster a level of personal control and perspective that allows them to negotiate relationships and situations with wisdom, rather than with the heat of anger.

GROWING OUR EMOTIONAL INTELLIGENCE

Most of us can grow our emotional intelligence. I say "most" because the starting place in EQ growth is a willingness and ability to recognize EQ issues in our lives. Those who are willing to face those problems can take steps toward greater health. In the absence of personal honesty and openness, growth will not occur.

It starts with understanding ourselves as best we can—our strengths, weaknesses, and wiring. We must understand how we respond to conflict, how open we naturally are, what triggers anger or defensiveness, how we are perceived by others, and how our actions impact others. Self-knowledge is the most important knowledge we can ever possess as leaders because it allows us to understand and modify our natural tendencies when those tendencies are unhealthy.

This means doing the hard work of understanding our shadow side—those tendencies that hurt our leadership if not modified. For instance, I know that I can out-debate almost anyone if I choose. While I might win the argument, this is not a great way to lead, so I work very hard to counter that tendency through KMS (Keep Mouth Shut) self-talk. I will literally repeat "KMS" to myself in meetings when I am tempted to say too much too quickly. I have been known to write it on a sticky note on the table in front of me when starting a potentially contentious meeting.

I repeat "nothing to prove, nothing to lose" to myself when someone chooses to take shots at me—it prevents me from shooting back (usually). Even though I have strong gifts in organizational leadership and can quickly see a reasonable way to proceed, I work very hard to listen and work the process so that others don't feel run over.

As we've seen before, a key factor in understanding ourselves is asking for and receiving honest feedback. I annually ask key staff if I do anything as a leader that disempowers them or that they wish I would do differently. Healthy leaders have nothing to lose by asking. Besides, they understand that it is not about them but about the team and the mission. Unhealthy leaders will never ask. Have you asked for feedback from those you lead? Are you willing to?

Questions to help us understand ourselves:

- What are the situations where my buttons get pushed and I respond in destructive ways?
- Who has permission to give me honest feedback on issues of my leadership or character?
- What does my spouse say about my shadow side?
- In what ways do my personal insecurities affect my leadership style?
- Are there issues that I know my staff would not feel comfortable talking to me about because I don't give permission?
- Do I have any relationships with unresolved problems that I have not tried my best to resolve?
- About which issues am I most defensive? Why?
- How would I describe my shadow side?
- How would I describe my ability to resolve conflict?

FLEXIBILITY

Leaders with high EQ are both self-defined and flexible. Their self-definition becomes a compass directionally, but within that direction they are highly flexible. For Jeff, leadership is telling others what they will do and getting his way. For healthy leaders, the direction setting process includes other key stakeholders, leaving flexibility for them to choose strategies that will take the organization that direction.

In most situations where leaders are inflexible and need to get their own way, the inflexibility is not worth the effort it requires or the problems it causes. God's design of church leadership as a team is based on the value of the counsel of multiple wise leaders.

Many of the conflicts in which leaders find themselves are a direct result of either poor self-definition or inflexibility to negotiate a common course of action. The leader who is self-defined while also engaged in healthy relational dialogue is a master at flexibly helping other good people come to a common strategy that allows the ministry to move in the preferred direction. Black-and-white individuals tend to polarize rather than bring people together.

HEALTHY EQ

I am a much more flexible, emotionally healthy person at fifty-seven than I was at twenty-seven. The key is to understand the major role that emotional intelligence plays in our leadership success and to pay attention to the EQ side of our lives. Those who do find that their ministry effectiveness increases over the years as they mature. Those who don't find themselves fighting the same battles over and over, unaware that they are caused by unhealthy EQ, not by some version of spiritual warfare or by bad people.

At the beginning of this chapter we listed signs of low EQ. Here are some signs of high EQ—targets for us as we seek to grow in our leadership effectiveness.

- I am approachable and have a nothing-to-prove-nothing-to-lose attitude.
- I seek to resolve conflict quickly and well.
- I am self-defined but always leave the door open for dialogue with those who disagree, and I work to preserve the relationships.
- I live with self-confidence but not hubris.
- I am highly flexible.
- I seek to understand myself well—my weaknesses, my strengths, and my shadow side.
- I ask others for feedback on my behaviors.
- I am a team player and value *us* more than *me*.
- I work hard to understand others and to put myself in their place.
- I don't hold grudges, and I extend forgiveness easily.
- I don't need to be popular, but I do desire to be respected.
- When conflict occurs, I take responsibility for my part.
- No issues are off-limits for my team to discuss.

- I am patient with people and always give them the benefit of the doubt.
- I don't take myself too seriously.

EMOTIONAL INTELLIGENCE AND DEEP INFLUENCE

Deep influence is the province solely of leaders who are personally secure and demonstrate emotional and relational health. Their health gives them credibility that goes far beyond that based on a position of authority. An ongoing commitment to learn how to lead out of healthy emotional intelligence will yield ever deeper influence.

Emotional intelligence and health is never fully achieved but is an ongoing journey for each of us in our flawed state. Whenever we recognize that our responses or actions are not what we would wish, we know we have an opportunity for growth. Every time we walk through conflict, we realize we have more to learn in dealing with other people.

Whenever there is a discrepancy between how we see ourselves and how others see us, we suffer a significant liability as leaders. While all of us are blind to some issues in our lives, some leaders choose not to listen to others regarding how they are perceived. The message threatens them, and they short-circuit their influence. Others are not drawn to defensiveness and dysfunction, but to nondefensiveness and health.

A study of the life, attitudes, and behaviors of Jesus is a study of the healthiest emotional intelligence we will ever find. It is worth studying the Gospels in that light and noting how

He interacted with people, how He treated them, and how He led them. I invite you on a quest to become the healthiest *you* that you can be so that your leadership and relationships reflect Christlike spiritual and emotional health.

For Reflection and Discussion

1. Look back over the list of warning signs of low EQ (pages 117-18) and the list of high EQ signs (pages 133-34). What are your emotional strengths? Which areas of emotional intelligence do you need to work on?

2. How do your low EQ issues impact your life or leadership in negative ways?

3. Who are the people in your life that can and do give you insight into your leadership as it relates to EQ?

4. Are there any relationships that you need to mend and that you can mend?

5. What steps can you take to grow your emotional intelligence on a regular basis?

CHAPTER SEVEN

LEADING FROM WHO GOD MADE *ME* TO BE

I am a leader. I am also a unique *me*. I am a unique *me* under construction, whom God has called to lead. But the only way I can lead is from who God made *me* to be. I cannot lead the way you do, and you cannot lead the way I do. We can learn from one another and become better leaders, but we can only lead effectively out of our individual design. When we try to lead like someone else, we short-circuit the very magic God hardwired into the individual for his or her best performance.

Leaders don't usually come into their own early in life for one simple reason: While the raw stuff may be there in youth, we don't yet really know who we are, how God wired us, what our sweet spot is, and just as important, what we are *not* good at. And time has not yet given us the lessons we must learn in order to fulfill our potential. Time is the leader's ally. Those in a hurry often make fatal errors. Those who are patient get the prize.

BIOGRAPHY AND LEADERSHIP

God knows what He is doing in preparing us for leadership. In 1956 I was the second-born of Gordy and Bonnie Addington. My father was already a civil engineer by training, had been to seminary, had planted a church, and was then in medical school preparing to go to the mission field. My mother, a teacher by training, was busy raising a young family that would encompass ten children.

At the age of four I remember flying on Pan Am to Hong Kong, where my parents were to serve for eleven years as medical missionaries. Hong Kong was a poor British colony teeming with refugees streaming in from China during the terrible years of the Cultural Revolution. When it was time to start school, I went to the local British school, Kowloon Junior.

At eleven I started to work at the hospital that my father cofounded with Dr. Robert Chapman. I worked in central supply, painted walls, and even assisted my father in surgery, where the one rule was, If you are going to faint, faint backward. Hong Kong was a fascinating place, full of people from all over the world, and I had the run of the colony with my siblings and friends. For high school I attended the now well-known Hong Kong International School with some thirty different nationalities represented. A poor missionary kid, I rubbed shoulders with kids who came to school in Daimlers, Mercedes-Benzes, and even Rolls-Royces.

It was obviously an international upbringing and education. Our home played host to sailors in port from the Vietnam War, businesspeople passing through, local friends, and any number of others. They all found their way to our large dinner table for a home-cooked meal.

I was a quiet, shy kid. I read voraciously. I took photos. I *never* thought of myself as a leader and had no inclination in that direction. I was an average student until I was kept back for a year and soared to the top of my class.

Every morning at five we would get up so the family could eat breakfast together, and then we would have devotions, reading a chapter of the Bible, working our way through book after book. I hated those early mornings, but learned the Bible nonetheless. At an early age, after special meetings in the church we attended, I gave my heart to Christ and over time came to believe that I would teach, preach, and write when I grew up. Leadership was not part of the equation.

Then the equation changed. I did not realize that third-culture kids often grow up faster and learn independence sooner than others. At fifteen I came back to the States, to the east side of St. Paul where "travel" meant going to Wisconsin to deer hunt and where many of my classmates' dads worked at the local breweries. Not only was I out of my element, but I stood out. I got kicked out of one class for arguing with the teacher about the Vietnam War (I believed I knew Asia better than he did). At church I quickly became the leader of the youth program. Having worked since I was eleven, I started a home-painting business and even employed fellow students, building on the painting skills honed at the hospital in Hong Kong. From the age of fifteen on, leading has been a consistent part of my story.

Our biographies are important because they are all part of the preparation for our most significant leadership roles as leaders. I am a product of an international upbringing, a deep love for Scripture and for the church, the independence of my childhood, and periods of suffering, as well as ministry successes and failures. It was during my late forties that my biography and my gifting converged, and I began to lead an international ministry organization.

CONVERGENCE

A reading of Scripture indicates that God is *not* in a hurry in crafting leaders. He is not concerned with age but rather with readiness. Think of Moses and his biography, handcrafted by God for his ultimate leadership role at the age of eighty. Or Nehemiah, handcrafted by God for his critical leadership role in rebuilding Jerusalem. God handcrafted David for his role in large part in the years when he was harassed and chased by Saul. Part of the leader's preparation over time is honing of leadership skill, while much of it is cultivation of heart character.

Convergence happens when all of one's biography, wiring, experience, and handcrafting come together in a leadership role made for the individual, in a role in which he or she will make maximum contribution to God's kingdom. Convergence is when one knows, *This is what I was made for!* It does not come easily, and it only comes when we are ready.

Leading well involves a series of opportunities to grow. For me it started at age sixteen, when I became the leader of my youth group. When I went to the University of Minnesota, I became the leader of the commuter InterVarsity group. After seminary my task was leading a church, where my leadership was severely challenged and I came away deeply wounded. After several years of sabbatical from both leadership and full-time ministry I found myself at the national office of the EFCA, where I again started to pick up leadership responsibilities, eventually taking charge of ministry advancement and using my church experience to consult on church leadership and governance.

Each of these roles combined my prior experiences, good and bad, successful and unsuccessful, to bring a set of experiences and knowledge to my new role. But the greatest convergence came in 2004, when I stepped into the role of leading what is now called ReachGlobal, the international ministry of the EFCA, where my love for the world, my international upbringing, my organizational abilities, and my commitment to the church and its expansion all came together in a job made for me.

I am convinced that God knows exactly what He is doing as He crafts our leadership experiences for each leadership spot along the way, and often for an ultimate role where He will use all of those threads of life, experience, upbringing, wiring, failure, and success for our greatest kingdom influence. One only needs to look at biblical figures to see this at work: Moses, Joshua, David, Deborah, Nehemiah, Esther, Mary, or Paul.

It is worth taking the time to think through your personal biography and jot down the unique experiences you have had, the forces that shaped you, the strengths God has given you, and the leadership roles you have held. Each is a thread in the tapestry of your life that God weaves together as your leadership assignments and influence grow. Each of us is unique, created for a unique role that only he or she can fulfill, each in his or her distinctive way. As Paul wrote to the Ephesians, we were "created in Christ Jesus for good works, which God prepared beforehand *so that we would walk in them*" (Ephesians 2:10, NASB, emphasis added). Your role was created just for *you*. It is not just a job; it was crafted before your birth for *you* to fulfill in the unique ways that only *you* can. And along the way, God handcrafted *you* to fill that role. This is true today, and it will be true tomorrow.

If God's hand has brought us to where we are, we should enjoy a high view of our responsibility in the roles we currently have. *If* God has matched us so well to our roles, we should face each day in leadership with diligence, seriousness, energy, and faith. This is *not* just a job, it is a divine appointment. And so we can trust that God will give us what we need to carry out the task. That confidence is a great help on those days when we ask, *Why am I here?*

We should not underestimate God's sovereignty in connecting us wisely with the right assignment at the right time, as long as we remain sensitive to His direction. Our commitment to His agenda will bring His blessing. Pursuing *our* agenda in spiritual leadership roles rarely brings His blessing.

UNIQUELY CALLED AND QUALIFIED

Leadership roles are not generic. In successful leadership, there is a unique fit between the experience and wiring of the leader and the unique needs of the organization or the part of the organization he or she is leading. This is why it is critical that we understand both our gifting and our experience from our biographies *and* that we remain deeply sensitive to God's leading in our lives.

As a young leader I assumed that, on the basis of my leadership gifts, I could probably lead almost anything. I now know that, not only is that not true, but I would not be happy in many leadership situations because they don't fit my wiring or experience. As I have been sensitive to God's leading, He has directed my feet to places where He wanted me, where there was a fit for me, and where I could make a unique contribution at that point in time. Had I, rather than God, been in charge of my leadership trajectory, I fear I would have missed the mark!

I am always amused at God's creativity. I have been at the national office of the EFCA now for twenty-five years. It is the *last* place I ever intended to be. After my dark night of the soul in the pastorate, I took two years off and sold furniture.

It fed my family, for which I was deeply grateful, but the work did not feed my soul. Restless, I considered law school. I really did not know what I was going to do.

I received a call from the then-president of the EFCA indicating that he was looking for an assistant. The catch was that he had only one year left in his term and would be retiring. It presented me with a dilemma. On the one hand, I was restless and needed a new challenge. On the other hand, I had not been served well in my pastorate by some denominational officials who could have helped, and the last thing I wanted to be was a "denominational bureaucrat" (my view). I accepted the opportunity, assuming that I would only be there one year, and then I would be gone when the president retired.

Does God have a sense of humor? I cannot imagine any other way I would have ended up in a denominational leadership role—one that was custom-made for me—involving a variety of responsibilities that allowed me to write, consult with local churches, influence the international church, and now lead the international mission ReachGlobal. God knew what I did not know, and He directed my path in ways that I could not have foreseen. In His creativity, He saved me from opportunities that were not right for me and allowed my influence to grow in positions that were handcrafted for me.

Take a moment to think through the unforeseen curves your leadership trajectory has taken, and consider how God's invisible hand has directed your path to where you are today. The Scripture I memorized as a child is correct in ways that I could never have imagined then: "Trust in the LORD with all your heart and lean not on your own understanding; in all your ways submit to him, and he will make your paths straight" (Proverbs 3:5-6).

This leads me to a fundamental leadership principle: *God knows where we will be most influential, most satisfied, most productive, and most effective.* He knew, for instance, that I needed a role that involved international work—that was His purpose for my international upbringing. *He also knows the leadership and life lessons we must walk through in order to become the leaders He wants us to become.* His path can be trusted even when life is confused and the future unknown. Life never turns out the way we think it will when we are young. But if we will follow carefully, He will lead us to the unique places that were made for us. Where we allow our own agenda and ambition to get in the way, we will likely take hard and unnecessary detours.

The constant prayer of those who desire to exercise deep influence for Christ should be that God would direct our paths in those ways that will make deep influence possible. Our prayers will be answered in unlikely ways, but they will be answered. We will discover roles that are uniquely made for us and where we will be most successful.

UNDERSTANDING OUR LIFE THEMES

Over time, our lives reveal predicable life themes that reveal ways that God has wired us and passions that He has given us. These are divinely implanted and point to the unique role that God wants us to play in His work. Understanding those themes helps us understand ourselves and the roles in which we are likely to be successful and satisfied.

My own life themes include the following:

- I simplify complexity.
- I integrate theology into life and ministry.
- I am wired to clarify organizational structures.
- I love strategic leadership.
- I work to raise up the next generation of leaders.
- I live with deep intentionality.
- I want to see all of God's people released for maximum ministry.
- I am passionate about God-centered living.
- I care deeply for and love the global church.

What these themes mean is that if I am going to be most satisfied and productive, I need a role that allows me to live out these passions. Some of them I can fulfill in any role. Others require a specific role, and to the extent that I cannot live one or more of these passions out, I will be restless.

If you are living with a significant degree of restlessness in your current role, it would be worthwhile to think about your own life themes. If your themes reveal passions that you are not currently living out, it would be well to find ways that you can engage those themes in your current position, either formally or informally. If they cannot be engaged in your current role, you might need to pray about a new role in which your passions and wiring can be fulfilled.

In my own case, if my task doesn't involve an international component, I become restless. Years ago my son Jon humorously told people that I was driven to leave the continent every six months, whether I had a reason or not. Likewise, given my wiring to clarify organizational structures and simplify complexity, I need the challenge of leading a relatively complex organization.

This self-examination is not a self-centered pursuit. It is about how God chose to wire us, the unique passions He chose to give us—all because of the unique role He wants each of us to play in His kingdom. My themes are unique. Your themes are unique. Each of us plays a unique role in His work, and together the symphony of the themes of many make up the wonderful mix of gifting that advances His agenda in our world.

Neither financial remuneration nor status can make up for the satisfaction of being in a place where we can live out those causes that we care about and were wired for. When we can live according to our life themes, we exist in our sweet spot. Much life dissatisfaction, restlessness, and frustration come from not being in the right spot!

In our own organization we place a huge emphasis on helping people discover their wiring and passions (their themes) and then finding roles that fit their unique experience and gifting. Many times, what may look like incompetence is simply the wrong job fit for the unique wiring God gave.

Just as we are unique in our gifting and wiring, so are all those who work in our organizations. Part of our leadership stewardship is developing a culture where we do all we can to get all people into roles that bring them fulfillment and where they will be most successful. Sometimes this will mean helping them find roles elsewhere, hard as that is, if we cannot find a compatible role within the organization. Our philosophy in ReachGlobal is that we will do all that we can to keep our personnel growing, engaged, and in positions compatible with their wiring.

LEADERSHIP STYLE AND INDIVIDUAL DESIGN

You are unique, and so is your leadership style. There are always ways that we can become healthier leaders, but we will always lead in ways that are consistent with how God created us.

This is important because many of us look at other leaders and seek to emulate their leadership style. After all, they have been successful and we want to be successful. We read their books on leadership to understand how we can lead better, but the reality is that most leaders can only describe how *they* lead; they cannot tell us how *we* should lead. The best books on leadership describe universal leadership principles or help leaders understand themselves and their impact on others. No book can define a leadership style that will work best for you because you will lead out of the unique ways that God gave you.

Think about the great leaders in Scripture. Moses was a spiritualist who led out of his intimate relationship with

God. Nehemiah was a strategist who could look at a situation, figure out what was needed, and quickly make a plan. Joshua was a commander and led like one. Barnabas was an encourager and deeply relational, while Paul was a driver and deeply strategic. Timothy was a shy leader who needed Paul's encouragement not to be bowled over by strong personalities. Esther led behind the scenes, using wisdom as her strategy.

What we should never do is compare our leadership to that of others. We can learn from others, but we will never be exactly like anyone else. God made us who we are for a reason, and He actually likes the way He made us. This is not an excuse not to grow our abilities. It is to recognize that God made each of us with intentional design and that to try to be something else is to deny that His creation was good.

This is something to remember when you come under fire from those who don't appreciate how God wired you. One of the realities of leadership is that some people you lead won't want to be led by you. They may critique your spirituality or competence when in reality they just don't like your leadership style. We ought to do all that we can to stay relationally connected in these instances, but in the end we cannot be what we were not created to be.

As a pastor I remember how painful it was when someone left the church because he or she did not like my style. A few vociferous voices nipped at my heels for years after coming into ReachGlobal. They were like pit bulls. Nothing I did satisfied them. They felt free to share their unhappiness with others, both inside and outside of the organization. They considered me deeply unspiritual and unqualified to lead. All leaders face situations like these at one time or another. The higher our visibility, the more it will happen. We will never be all things to all people.

In my chapter on emotional intelligence I spoke of the need to be self-defined—to be clear about who we are and the position we take while remaining relationally connected with those who may not agree with us. A part of self-definition is knowing one's own leadership style and being comfortable in one's own skin. We lead with humility, high EQ, and sensitivity but also with an unapologetic attitude about how God chose to wire us for leadership.

In addition, if we build strong teams around us and if those on our leadership teams are on the same page, we can have confidence that the criticism is not really about us but about those who are unhappy. I believe that if staff cannot serve with a happy heart and a clear conscience, they really need to serve elsewhere, where they can.

God chooses a person to lead at a particular time for a particular purpose that matches up with his or her unique wiring. While my predecessor and I have many of the same convictions, we lead very differently. I stand on his shoulders in many ways, but times change, organizations go through transitions, and I serve as a transitional leader. Whoever comes after me will lead in his or her unique way for a unique purpose as well. Moses was a leader for the Exodus, Joshua for taking the land, David for unifying Israel.

Coming into my present leadership position in ReachGlobal,

I knew that, since I represented major but needed change, I needed to be absolutely confident that it was God's will for me to take the position. There was too much at stake both for the organization and for me. Mary Ann and I asked God to show us beyond a shadow of a doubt that He wanted us there and would bless my leadership. Through an amazing series of events that were impossible to anticipate or orchestrate, He made it clear that this was His doing. That clarity has given me confidence through some tough times—confidence that He put me here for this season and that I can trust Him to go before me. Indeed He has in a remarkable way.

STRENGTHENING OUR LEADERSHIP THROUGH TEAM

It is precisely because we are so individually wired that building the best and strongest team around us is so important. In my book on teams, *Leading from the Sandbox*, I define a high-impact team as "a group of missionally aligned and healthy individuals working strategically together under good leadership toward common objectives, with accountability for results."[1]

Leaders are architects for the organization or for the part of the organization they lead. Architects are conceptual thinkers who connect ideas, opportunities, resources, and strategies in order to build the best ministry infrastructure possible. But architects don't build the building; they bring into the picture general contractors and subcontractors (other leaders) and work together with them to bring the idea to reality.

While I have the ability to envision the future and to craft a ministry philosophy that will get us to the goal, I need process-oriented folks who can develop the systems and structures necessary and the specialists who can develop pieces of the ministry. Leaders who think they can do it alone are fooling themselves in a big way, and they limit the growth of the ministry to their own span of control or gifting.

Healthy leaders are unthreatened by other strong leaders. This makes them able and willing to build strong, results-oriented, aligned teams, not limited to their own abilities but multiplying their span of gifting (and therefore their ministry opportunity) in an exponential way. In the organization I lead, for instance, I have twelve senior team members and approximately fifty key leaders in an organization of 550. My leadership ability is multiplied by those fifty key leaders, and it is we together who provide leadership for the organization.

This also means that my leadership style, highly strategic and results-oriented, is balanced by the many other leadership styles of our key leaders. Some are more relational than I, some more process-oriented, some more detail-friendly. In that way my wiring, unique to me and necessary to the organization at this time in our history, is not the only leadership style but is balanced by those who have much different styles than I, who are strong leaders in their own right. This balance gives an organization the upside of a strong directional leader but mitigates the downsides of his or her leadership style. Any individual leader, alone, is limited by his or her span of control or gifting. Wise leaders multiply that span for the sake of the health, depth, breadth, and growth of the ministry.

The prerequisite for building this kind of team is a leader who is willing not only to gather around them other strong leaders but also to empower them to lead in their area without micromanaging their work. Lack of empowerment will cause good leaders to look for other ministry opportunities where they can actually use all of their skills and gifting.

To make this work, the ministry philosophy must be clear regarding the organization's mission, guiding principles, central ministry focus, and culture. Clarity in these four areas provides the guidance and boundaries for everyone in leadership and therefore allows for significant empowerment and accountability at all levels of the organization.

In the absence of clarity, other leaders don't know what their boundaries are and therefore either act first and ask for forgiveness later or fail to act without permission. Neither course is a healthy course for any organization.

Many leaders feel a need to control others as a means of protecting their influence. They make it all about them! Yet ironically, control does just the opposite and limits their influence. The more I empower others to extend the reach of the ministry I lead, the more influence I (and we together) have. The way to kingdom influence is through empowering rather than controlling others.

Any leader concerned about deep influence will empower as many others as possible in order to make the greatest impact. After all, people of deep influence understand the priority is the mission and *not* them. Their role is to facilitate the mission and to empower the right people. It is a stewardship role on behalf of Christ for the advancement of *His* agenda.

THINKING BEYOND OURSELVES

If God has us in our leadership roles for a reason, and if He wants to use our gifts and wiring to influence the organization we lead, it stands to reason that He also wants to plant the DNA of the best we bring deep into the culture of the ministry in a way that will outlast our tenure as leaders. That means that we must think beyond ourselves, and even beyond our tenure, to leave behind something that is lasting, significant, and effective. Our tenure is a long-term investment in the future of the ministry we lead! The measure of our leadership is not primarily what happens when we are leading, but what we leave behind.

This goes beyond thinking day to day. It is about thinking of the future and whether those things that God has brought us to accomplish will have a compelling influence after we are gone. Even though I am a transitional leader in my organization, I am deeply thankful for the lasting influence of my predecessor. His passion was to see the mission expand its influence hugely and to see the Holy Spirit empower this ministry. I have brought changes in philosophy and methodology, but the best of what he brought will long outlast him. I will always honor that legacy and seek to build on it.

A key to understanding organizations is to know that they

are slow to change. It's part of human nature. Those who are familiar with the "change curve" know that the percentage of innovators and early adapters is modest compared to those who are middle or late adapters or laggards. Most people will seek to understand and cooperate with leaders, but their thinking and methodology can quickly revert back to the comfortable and "normal" if a new DNA is not planted deep in the organization.

For leaders who bring change and desire that change to last, there are two tipping points to watch. The first tipping point is a change in thinking. One of the significant changes we have been working on in ReachGlobal is for our staff to be equippers of others rather than primarily doers. In this way we move from a model of addition in missions to a model of multiplication. For those who came into the organization when staff were primarily doers, this has been a difficult transition to make, but ten years in we have passed the tipping point in thinking multiplication rather than addition.

The second and more difficult tipping point is that of figuring out *how to do* multiplication rather than addition. Until that occurs, the new DNA will not have been planted in a way that will outlast our current leadership. It is really about developing, empowering, and releasing others in ministry. As *that* concept catches momentum, the DNA of being equippers will become part of the lasting culture of ReachGlobal.

As we have redefined the mission, guiding principles, central ministry focus, and preferred culture of our organization, we have constantly asked the hard questions of ourselves:

How deep have the changes gone, and how consistent are our actions with our ministry philosophy? Further, we are always working with our leaders to figure out how to best drive the preferred DNA the deepest into the organization. It takes a full-court press by all of leadership to ensure alignment and delivery on our promise.

Simply managing the status quo is not leading. If God has called us to lead, He has done so for a reason. It is *our* responsibility to think about what it is that God wants us to implant and leave behind. Having answered that question, we need to ensure that our contribution becomes part of the culture of the ministry we lead. And we need to do it through a high-impact team in which the gifts of the group outweigh the gifts of any one leader.

For leaders thinking about transitioning to a new ministry or being asked to consider a new leadership role, a good question to ask both the new organization and oneself is, what is the unique role I can fill, given my gifting and wiring and the needs of this organization? It is not enough to engage in a new leadership challenge. The leader must fulfill a role that is consistent with the needs of the organization and the gifting of the leader.

PLANNING FOR SUCCESSION

The moment I was elected to my current leadership position, I knew that I needed to start thinking of who would succeed me. That may seem a curious thought on my first day in my new role, but I knew that unless I could provide continuity, my time and effort would be short-circuited. The best for the organization requires thinking beyond one's own tenure and planning in order to sustain momentum and healthy direction. This avoids the wild swings that organizations often experience at points of leadership change.

Succession is a high-value priority for leaders of deep influence, because they desire to sustain the health that they have brought to the organization and they allow their successor to build on that health. We want to leave the organization *better* than when we inherited it and pass it off to someone who can take it to the next level of effectiveness.

If at all possible, each of us should have one or more individuals who could lead the organization short-term if we are incapacitated and one or more who could lead the organization long-term should we leave. To fail to develop such leadership is to short-circuit our own leadership investment and potentially to see our work undone when we are gone.

This is all part of the long-term perspective of leaders who understand that their leadership is a trust from God to be managed on His behalf for the missional effectiveness of the ministry. We are stewards, not owners!

Passing the baton in a healthy manner preserves the best influence we have had. My predecessor gave me this gift. When the search process for his successor began, he vowed to pray daily and to support fully whoever that successor would be, for the good of the organization. He did that amazingly well, and his generous spirit and care for the ministry enhanced the deep influence he had earned with

ReachGlobal. How we leave or transition is not only a measure of our character; it impacts our lasting influence.

WIRED FOR A PURPOSE

There are many things that I am not good at, but at the end of the day I have to trust the fact that God wired me the way He did for a specific reason, for a unique role. I will never be my leader, Bill, with his amazing relational ability. I will never be my former colleague, Steve, with his incredible detail and process gift. I will never be brilliant at making financial and business deals like my soul mate, Grant. I will never be as mercy-driven as my son Chip and my wife, Mary Ann, or as entrepreneurial as my son Jon. But God knew as much when He crafted me and intentionally gave me a unique biography, life themes that have described me for most of my life, and wiring that allows me to do what I do.

While I will never be content with the status quo in terms of my spiritual transformation or the development of my EQ and inner life, I *am* content with how God uniquely made me because I am God's "workmanship, created in Christ Jesus for good works, which God prepared beforehand so that [I] would walk in them" (Ephesians 2:10, NASB). I rest content in that fact. And so should you. Each of us has been wired for a divine purpose, and while we continue to grow into Christlikeness, we ought to be content with God's wiring and purpose for our lives.

Being comfortable with who God made us to be removes the need to pretend we are something we are not or to try to become what God did not make us to be. That comfort and security with His architecture of our lives leads to deep influence because it is only the most authentic version of a person that can have deep influence on others.

For Reflection and Discussion

1. How has your biography influenced the role you have today? Can you identify specific biographical events that molded you for your current job?

2. How would you identify your life themes? Does your current role allow you to live and work in alignment with those themes?

3. Jot down some unique characteristics of your leadership style. How is it different from that of other leaders you know? Are you comfortable with how God wired you to lead?

4. How does your leadership team strengthen your leadership? Do you have the right skills among your team's members?

5. What are you doing to plan for leadership succession?

CHAPTER EIGHT

CHOOSING INTENTIONALITY

Few issues more significantly separate a leader of deep influence from others than the choice to live with intentionality, rather than taking the easy route of accidental living. Everything we have considered thus far requires intentionality in the way we think about life, the choices we make, and the schedules we keep.

Becoming a person of deep influence is really about a series of life choices: what commitments we make, what priorities we focus on, how we spend our time, whom we spend time with, whether we understand God's call on our life, and whether we intentionally *chase* that call. Competing with these wise choices are the numerous distractions and options that present themselves to us.

A THEOLOGY OF TIME

When Scripture says, "Teach us to number our days" (Psalm 90:12), it reminds us of a profound truth. Our time is limited, and therefore how we spend it is important. Time is one of the only things that we cannot get more of. Money comes and goes, but time simply goes. Every day that passes is one day closer to eternity and a day that we cannot do over.

Think how carefully we consider our financial investments and how we think through purchases, since for most of us money is in limited supply. If that is true with money, which fluctuates over the years, how much more true it is of time, which cannot be reclaimed. Wise individuals budget their money, prioritizing their spending. Wise leaders likewise budget their time and prioritize their allocation of that irreplaceable resource.

For leaders, time is the most precious commodity, and every time we say yes to something we implicitly say no to something else. That means that if we agree to something that is *good* but not *essential*, we have eliminated opportunities to give time to the *essential*. Leaders cannot overestimate the value of their time and the importance of evaluating the choices they have, given their limited hours.

Because we do not think of time like money, we often do not think carefully about time we give away. Someone needs "just a moment," someone else asks us to attend a meeting, and another would like to have us at a conference. All good things, perhaps, but if we were being asked for money, we would not quickly say yes but would want to think and pray about it, because our money is limited and we only want to invest it in important things. So also with our time: Thinking of time like money makes one realize that every hour, every meeting, every trip, every day we give away is an investment and, given the nature of time, an expensive one.

Time is precious, and often the very fact that leaders are not disciplined in their use of time at work compromises their ability to be present with their spouses, families, or friends. To say nothing about what our schedules often do to time we spend with Jesus, to whom all of our energy should be dedicated in the first place. Never underestimate the implications of choices regarding time. For people of influence it matters.

POWERFUL CHOICES

Given the premise that time is our most precious commodity, the choices we make about how we invest it become powerful choices that determine much of our effectiveness. Therefore it's important to discern what God has called each of us uniquely to do, what we have *not* been called to do, and what *others* can do instead of us.

This requires us to know with a fair amount of precision what our central priorities are. I currently serve as a senior vice president of the EFCA with oversight of our international mission, ReachGlobal. In that role I have five primary priorities:

- to help provide overall leadership to the EFCA movement,

- to write for the national and international church,
- to provide vision and missional clarity to ReachGlobal,
- to mentor leaders in ReachGlobal and movement leaders internationally, and
- to mobilize people and financial resources.

These are the things that I *must* do. Our ReachGlobal senior team is giving leadership to many other priorities, but I take responsibility for these. Being clear about our personal priorities as leaders is critical. Those priorities are the grid through which we filter decisions from among the many time options in front of us. Foggy priorities yield foggy decisions. Focused priorities allow us to focus our time and energy in the direction of our core responsibilities.

The priorities we choose should be consistent with both our calling and our wiring. And they should reflect the highest use of our gifting, rather than those things that we could do in a mediocre way. Focusing on the highest use of our gifting increases our influence.

Knowing what I am called to do means that I must empower others to do what they have been called to do. It means that, within well-defined boundaries, I stay *out* of their way and don't manage what they are leading. If I meddle in their responsibilities, I disempower them and take away precious time from my key responsibilities. I can keep current with my senior leaders with a monthly check-in, but if I need to second-guess their decisions or work, either I have problems empowering others or I have the wrong leaders.

Sometimes this means not involving ourselves in decisions within the purview of others, even if asked—not out of lack of interest but because our time is limited and we have full faith in their ability to make decisions in their areas of responsibility. This does not mean that we are not available to our team. But we may not always be available in the *way* that others desire us to be available. Intentional leaders do not allow others to make their time decisions for them.

Since I know what my key priorities are, the bulk of my time is invested in those five areas. I do not allow distractions to regularly pull me away from these priorities. Saying yes to an activity or commitment is like writing a time check. Each check written takes time out of my time bank that I cannot get back. So choosing which checks to write is an important discipline.

The two most powerful words in our lives are *yes* and *no*. What we say yes to gives us opportunity to fulfill God's mandate for our lives. What we graciously say no to *also* gives us opportunity to fulfill God's mandate for our lives! Both words allow us to focus on what God has called us to do and to avoid distractions from the same. My tendency is to say yes too often and to say no too seldom. Both tendencies hurt me—and, I suspect, many others.

I will often talk over requests and opportunities with a trusted colleague and with my wife before accepting those that will take significant time out of my schedule. I know how prone I am to accept something that is good but that is not best for fulfilling God's calling. My confidants often ask the right questions and provide a more objective read on the importance of the request.

In evaluating requests for our time we need to take into account the actual cost of the request. An invitation to speak might sound like a small cost, but add to that the preparation and travel time and the cost suddenly goes up.

With all the requests, options, and expectations that descend on leaders, all competing for their time, how do we determine when to say yes or no in order to keep our sanity and fulfill our destiny? Here are some simple questions we can ask as a grid for our thinking:

- Is this opportunity in line with my key priorities?
- If I say yes, will it detract from what I really *must* do?
- Is *my* presence really needed?
- Could someone else do this rather than me?
- If my time was worth two thousand dollars per day, would this be worth that time?
- If I accept this commitment, what other commitments will suffer?

In my book, *Leading from the Sandbox*, I lay out a paradigm for establishing key result areas (top priorities) and an annual ministry plan to fulfill them. The discipline of that process guides time choices for me and for everyone in our organization. It helps us live intentionally rather than accidentally.

Ironically, the more intentional we are about how we live,

the more time we have for the people who need us, for emergencies, and for inner life and family. Intentional people may be busy people, but they don't need to be harried people. A harried routine can make us feel important, but it rarely makes us effective.

DISTRACTION MANAGEMENT

Distractions are the leaks in our commitment to intentional living. They cause us to leak time, energy, and influence. Someone has said that if the Evil One cannot convince us to sin, he will tie us up with distractions. Either distractions manage us or we manage them. And unless actively managed, they *will* manage us.

Distraction management begins with the realization that our attention can easily be diverted from what we really need to do. In fact, we might secretly welcome them as diversions from doing more difficult or important things. Managing distractions is not about avoiding people or being unresponsive to legitimate demands on our attention. It is about being prepared with a plan to manage what otherwise becomes a deadly drain on the priorities we must fulfill.

Cell Phones Have Voice Mail

For many of us our primary number is our cell number. Few people call my office number (only those who don't know me) and no one calls my home number (I don't have one). Welcome to the efficiency of communication and one of the greatest distractions of all.

Fortunately, we have voice mail and caller ID. When spending focused time on one of your priorities, avoid answering the phone unless the person calling is on your "can disturb" list (I have about twenty of those). Chances are that when you listen to the voice mail, you will be glad you waited.

Schedule Phone Appointments

I am accessible to anyone who has a valid reason to talk to me. What I am not available for are random phone calls (unless one is on my "can disturb" list). I intentionally set aside time in my week for phone appointments, which are scheduled by my administrative assistant, Missy, for a specific time and a specific amount of time. That way I am accessible, but I have control over my time.

Use a Gatekeeper

Not everyone has this luxury, but if you have an assistant, use him or her to vet calls and requests for appointments. Here is the truth: Many people want a piece of a leader, but not everyone should get face time. If someone calls, Missy will find out who he or she is and why that person is calling. She will often know whether I or someone else should take the call. If someone else, she will route the call to the right person. If in doubt, she will talk to me and then schedule either an in-person or phone appointment accordingly.

Because my assistant knows my personal priorities, I give her permission to tell me honestly if she thinks that I don't need to be in a meeting or to say yes to a request. I have always been blessed with confident, assertive, and helpful assistants who speak their mind and "manage up" very well.

Schedule E-mail

I receive in excess of one hundred e-mails on a given day. Since I am committed to responding to any e-mail from my worldwide staff, I need to schedule specific time when I pay attention to e-mail and time when I ignore it in order to get something else done. I also give my assistant access to my e-mail account so that she can respond to issues that don't need my attention. Generally I will schedule e-mail time during the periods of the day when I will not be as productive—afternoons—so that I save the best hours for the most significant activities.

The "Open" Door

Sometimes my door is not open! I may be in a meeting or engaged in something that requires my focus. Indiscriminate open-door policies are nice but not very effective, if the result is constant interruptions. I am always available to my senior team if they really need me, but by scheduled appointment— whether five minutes or an hour—is usually the way we meet.

Skype

Travel is a time killer, and I travel a lot. But I am also realizing that there are times when an Internet meeting will be as effective as physically meeting face-to-face. On the Internet one can still talk face-to-face and save money, energy, and time—resources that can be invested elsewhere. I still travel, but I now ask the question, *Is there an alternative?*

The Coffee Shop

For many of us the office is the last place where we get *our* work done. I schedule days when my assistant can put appointments on my calendar. When I am in the office I am pretty accessible. I then schedule blocks of hours, entire days, and sometimes a block of days when I work either from home, at the coffee shop, or at a remote office for projects requiring uninterrupted concentration.

Block Scheduling

Block scheduling is a simple tool that can help us manage distractions. Rather than doing five things at once and allowing phone, e-mail, and people to constantly interrupt, it's sometimes best to block several hours or longer to focus on one task. Block scheduling takes discipline, but it is far more productive than juggling numerous issues at once.

Communicate with Your Team on What Works Well for You

As part of playing to your strengths, it is always helpful to have a dialogue with your team on what works best for you in terms of your productivity. I have found that teams I've led have been very flexible and even encouraging of those techniques that allow me to lead better, use my time wisely, and serve them well. They will help you if they know what you need in order to be effective.

Schedule Proactively and Ahead

Our calendars are the way we connect the compass (our priorities) with the clock (our time management). A number of components make up our schedules. First are our ongoing obligations. These are the nonnegotiable, routine meetings that are part of the rhythm of the organization or team you lead. They go on your calendar first.

Second are the high priorities that must be accomplished over the course of the next months or year. Because these are the tasks that *must* be done in order for you to be effective as a leader, they get blocked out next on your calendar. Because one of my five priorities is writing, I will block days or even weeks when that is all that is on my schedule (still allowing time to keep up with day-to-day concerns).

Included in this second category should be the time we need to think, read, and consider issues important to the organization, team, or ministry we lead. Unless we specifically schedule "think time," we will probably not get it. And this time is perhaps some of the most important time for leaders of deep influence.

Just as think time is so important, those activities that recharge us emotionally, physically, and spiritually are also key components of a healthy life. They need to be scheduled in so that we don't lose our edge. For me these include time for resting, reading, fly fishing, and chainsaw therapy on some acreage we have. For many years, my family has simply kept the month of August completely free for rest.

Third are times when we just need to be available for our team or for appointments—by phone or in person. I block "office days" on my calendar so that my assistant can schedule face time with those who need it.

Fourth comes everything else, but notice that the key is to schedule in order of priority. The alternative is that the less important will often crowd out the more important, allowing slow leakage and ultimately exhaustion of our effectiveness and influence. While this kind of scheduling limits our options (we cannot live by the seat of our pants), it helps us use our time with greater discipline and intentionality.

Factored into our schedules should be enough margin to deal with the unexpected. With some margin, schedules can be rearranged when necessary without losing time for the four components above.

Prayerfully consider your calendar—it is the checkbook for your most important resource: time. That is why I give my calendar so much attention. I will often "think gray" about requests or opportunities and pray about them as I consider the next three to six months of my schedule. Thinking gray (postponing a decision) allows me to think through the ramifications of the time check I am thinking of writing and whether it is the right thing for me at this time, given my other obligations.

When I say yes too quickly too often, I end up tired and depleted and the truly important things suffer. Thus I am constantly looking at my calendar—sometimes with trusted colleagues or my wife—in order to make the very best time investment decisions possible because that is tied directly to my ability to exercise deep influence.

When Present, Be Fully Present

Intentionality with our calendar means that we are not always available for everyone. This is a reality of leadership, especially as our responsibilities grow. One way to compensate for this and to continue to be seen as available and approachable is to find times when you *can* be available. For instance, I know a pastor of a large church who stays around after the Sunday morning service until everyone who wants to see him has done so. While it may be hard to schedule a meeting with him during the week, anyone who wants to talk to him on Sunday can do so.

PERSONAL DEVELOPMENT

A key distinction of people of deep influence is that they have a lifelong passion for personal and professional development. They are intentional about growth because they are driven by the desire to have influence for God.

The main enemy of ongoing development is often laziness or complacency—that is, choosing to settle for what *is* rather than what *could be*. When Paul talked about forgetting the past and pressing into the future and running the race as one who wants to win the prize (see Philippians 3:12-14), he was speaking the language of those who are always reaching for a way to accomplish more and are never satisfied with where they are. This is not about being driven but about being intentional for the sake of our personal and ministry influence on behalf of Christ.

Our Mentors

All of us need mentors, and the wisest of us have multiple mentors since no one person is capable of providing everything we need. Personally, I have a set of people I consider informal mentors in my life, each of whom speaks from a different and wise perspective, and all of whom are people of deep influence to me.

These are people I deeply respect and trust, and from whom I learn each time I am with them. These are relationships based on friendship, all two-way relationships in which iron sharpens iron. I choose those friendships carefully and nurture them often.

I schedule monthly phone calls with some leaders, whom I respect and know, and we simply talk through mutual issues that we face. From the give-and-take of those conversations each of us usually leaves with something new to consider.

Mentors can also be "specialists" we engage for a specific issue we are facing in our leadership, or they can be ongoing coaches for a period of time to help us through a transition or simply to help us grow in a specific area. I serve as a mentor to a number of people on a monthly basis or as desired, mainly helping people think through options and ask the right questions.

Even if it means hiring a mentor to help you grow in a specific area, if that mentor has expertise, it is well worth the financial investment if it launches you to the next level of effectiveness. People of deep influence are always seeking leverage, and a coach or consultant can provide significant leverage and expertise in a short amount of time.

Discerning Areas of Specific Growth

Leaders usually have an intuitive sense about areas where they need to grow. Intentional development means that we don't ignore those areas but we have a plan for how we will press into them. All of us should be able to identify a handful of areas where our growth could make a significant difference in our effectiveness. We can then look for ways that we can grow in one or two of those areas over the next year.

Consider asking your team from time to time what areas of needed growth they see for you. They know you well, and asking them for feedback honors your relationships and models an open, nothing-to-prove-nothing-to-lose attitude. By your vulnerability you will gain the respect of your team. It also gives you added credibility when you make suggestions to them. In our organization *personal development* is top priority, a required key result area that we review annually.

FLYING AT THE RIGHT ALTITUDE

Choosing intentionality is about the ability to fly at the appropriate altitude and stay there. This means consistently paying attention to the issues that *we*, the leaders, must pay attention to. Dipping down to a lower altitude than we should means allowing ourselves to become distracted, and in the process disempowering others and wasting precious time and opportunity.

I often tell my staff that if I am going to lead well, I need to be able to fly at fifty thousand feet, where I can see the horizon from all directions, think, plan, strategize, and consider the macro issues our organization faces. No one else will do that for me.

Part of my intentionality is to fly at my appropriate altitude and to empower others to fly at their altitudes, with minimal interference from me in their work. Because I have a monthly check-in with each of my key leaders, we have a chance to dialogue with one another over critical issues. My job as their leader is not to redo their work but to enable them to accomplish their responsibilities.

LEADER STANDARD WORK

Each of us as a leader has a set of responsibilities that only he or she can fulfill. I call this *leader standard work*. If those responsibilities are not carried out by the leader because of the press of activities, because of expectations, or simply because one has not prioritized well, the organization or team will suffer.

Because leader standard work comprises the most important activities, they are scheduled on the calendar first and are rarely changed. This includes key meetings that occur at the same time each month, preparation for those meetings (they will only be as good as the preparation), monthly check-ins with leaders who report to you, built-in think and evaluation time, evaluation of results, and so on. For pastors it would also include preparation time for messages.

My calendar in Microsoft Outlook is color coded to reflect my leader standard work, with the various other activities scheduled around it so that I can visually see how and where I am spending my time. This ensures that my most critical commitments are not neglected.

These responsibilities are supplemented by an *execution journal* built off of a spreadsheet that lists all of the tasks and projects for which I am responsible, along with the date they are due, the percentage of each task that has been finished, and the date it is completed. Every time I make a commitment, I place that commitment in the journal and color-code it so that I'm easily reminded of its priority. Every day I look at the execution journal so that commitments I have made don't fall between the cracks or fail to reach completion on time. When leaders don't keep their commitments, others will not either.

One of the secrets to keeping commitments is understanding that every time we agree to do something, we must build time into our calendars to fulfill that obligation. If time is not realistically available in the calendar, we should either decline the project or modify the date by which we promise to complete it.

PRAYER TEAMS

Deep influence is ultimately about the influence of Christ flowing out of our lives into the lives of others. The deepest influence is always spiritual influence, the character of God shining through us. It is His thinking becoming our thinking, His heart becoming our heart, His priorities becoming our priorities, and His relationships becoming our relationships.

As I have shared my story, you have seen how my prayer team has played a pivotal role in my development, courage, and leadership work. I cannot imagine doing what I do without the support of a group of intercessors. I take this so seriously that on almost all of my international trips I take a prayer partner with me; I need that person's insight and help.

As I described in chapter 3, I also have three prayer teams that regularly pray for my family and ministry. It is not unusual for me to shoot a quick e-mail to any one of these teams for prayer around a specific meeting or situation I face. In addition, most months I share my whole calendar with these teams so they can pray knowledgeably about where I am on any specific day.

After years of this practice, I am clear that the spiritual power that lies behind my leadership is the power of those prayer teams. Prayer is the key to any deep influence I have, and I am deeply grateful for each individual who has made a commitment to uphold me and my family in prayer.

But this continuous support requires an intentional investment on our part month by month, replenishing and communicating with our prayer teams. We give the teams not just lists of requests but also feedback on the results of their prayers. Appropriate transparency—appropriate to the team with which you are communicating—is also important. Authentic openness invites more prayer.

On a personal level, I am intentional about praying for three things on a daily basis. First, I pray for the empowerment of God's Spirit in my life. Eternal influence requires God's working in and through us. Second, I pray for divine wisdom to make decisions that are compatible with God's wisdom and that avoid stupid mistakes. Third, I pray for favor with people because leadership is all about people, and unless we are granted favor with them we don't have influence. I face every day and every important meeting with a quick prayer for these three gifts that only God can grant.

We can be intentional about many things, but if we are not intentional about raising up prayer on our behalf, we have shortchanged ourselves. In the beginning I was shy about asking for prayer, wondering, *Why would anyone want to pray for me?* No longer! God gives people the desire to pray for others. He gives that gift because He wants us to be people of deep influence—on His behalf.

A WAY OF THINKING

Each of us makes the choice as to whether he or she will live accidentally or intentionally. For people of deep influence, this is an easy choice. They are committed to maximizing their impact for Christ and their influence with others. The price of that influence is a life of intentionality where first things come first and where time is seen as an investment.

In our organization we ask our personnel to take a "personal retreat day" once a month to think through priorities, talk to God about opportunities, evaluate their top three priorities for the next month, and evaluate how we did with our three priorities from the past month. This is a day to realign our thinking, priorities, and calendar and to ensure that we are on track with what is most important in our lives. It is also the day most of our staff write their monthly prayer updates to their prayer teams.

Many of us would think, *I can't afford to take a day, or even part of a day, off each month for that kind of thing.* The reality is that we cannot afford *not* to do this, because by taking the time to think deeply and to focus well, we actually get *more* done than we would have otherwise. If we cannot name our three top priorities for the coming month, we have not done our work of thinking carefully about what we should be up to. For a complete explanation about how to integrate this kind of thinking into your life or organization, read my book, *Leading from the Sandbox.*

An advantage of living with significant intentionality is that we end up focusing on fewer things, and in the process of doing less we accomplish more. We have chosen to focus on those things that are most important. We have moved from activity (all of us are busy) to results (focusing on the important, not the merely urgent). Those who focus on fewer, more important things see the greatest results.

As I look back over my leadership career, I realize that in my youth I often ran too fast. Because I had a lot of energy, I could get away with it. Today I don't have that level of energy, but in living more intentionally I have more time and greater joy on the journey. Today I do less but accomplish more. I still struggle with the powerful choices, and I still need wisdom, but I am making better decisions more often as I consider each time check that I write.

The result is greater and deeper influence. Even the ability to take time to write this and other books is a step toward greater influence. I was able to cut through the chaff of life and focus on fewer, more important things.

Intentional living is a prerequisite way of thinking that leads to any deeper influence.

For Reflection and Discussion

1. What is your strategy for determining how you schedule your time? Can you clearly identify your key responsibilities, and are these reflected on your calendar?

2. In what areas are you doing well in terms of living intentionally? Where do you need to rethink your intentionality?

3. Where are you tempted to dip below your necessary leadership altitude, and how does it impact those who work for you?

4.   What is your decision-making process for saying yes or no to opportunities? Are you satisfied that you do this well?

5.   How do you evaluate whether you are paying attention to the most important things in your schedule? Do you need to modify your strategy for this?

CHAPTER NINE

THINKING LIKE A CONTRARIAN

People of deep influence know two things about conventional wisdom that others don't understand. First, that conventional wisdom is just that: conventional. And second, that it is not always wisdom. One of the chief differences between people of deep influence and others is that those of deep influence think like contrarians.

That does not mean that they have a contrarian attitude! It does mean that they do not simply accept conventional answers to life and ministry. Each of the chapters in this book requires a different way of thinking compared to the way that most people think. In fact, these concepts are largely countercultural.

I am not encouraging you to become a curmudgeon who is disagreeable for the sake of being disagreeable. I am referring to people who do not accept conventional wisdom indiscriminately, without question. Contrarians ask different and better questions, come to different and better conclusions, and are willing to go against the stream when godly wisdom calls for it.

Wise leaders understand that the way to breakthroughs is *not* found in unthinkingly doing things as we have done them in the past. Rather it is found in an openness to new ways of thinking and doing. Effective leaders are not satisfied with mere incremental gains—merely tweaking what we are doing today—but are constantly looking for ways to leapfrog into the future by making a quantum leap.

RETHINKING CONVENTIONAL WISDOM

I have never forgotten a poster that reads: "If you always do what you always did, you always get what you always got." People of deep influence understand that truth and don't want to settle for getting what they always got. They are never satisfied with the status quo but want better, more effective, and greater *return on mission*.

For example, in the past several decades conventional wisdom has assumed that if we do certain things in our churches, those things will result in mature believers. But recent studies have rocked the church world, revealing that this was indeed conventional, *but not wisdom*; the promised maturity among congregants is in short supply. There is today a massive effort underway to determine better ways to see spiritual transformation take place.

In another example, the church world has been dramatically changed in the past decade by *video venues*. Essentially these are services that use video feed from the main service location to other locations, either on church property or on distant campuses. When the idea was first proposed, people said, "No one will watch a message on video" (conventional wisdom). Today the practice is helping ministries grow all over the world using technology. It took a handful of church leaders who said, "I bet this will work. Let's try it."

The world of missions has been going through a significant transformation as well. One of the most significant transformations has been the shift in the missionaries' role from being primarily hands-on practitioners (they are the experts and do the ministry) to being primarily coaches and trainers (working alongside national leaders). Today Western missionaries function primarily to raise up and champion healthy national workers who, in most cases, can do better in their context than we can. That shift took place when a number of mission leaders started to ask if there was not a better way to reach a world that has exploded from 1.7 billion in 1900 to seven billion today.

There have been many such shifts that have changed the ministry landscape. But they always start with a leader who asks *why* things are done the way they are, thinks deeply, and comes up with a solution—radically different from conventional wisdom—that results in significant ministry advancement.

The path to contrarian thinking is characterized by these elements:

- Conventional wisdom is not simply accepted as wisdom.
- Current practices are always scrutinized for better ways.
- The questions *Why?* and *Why not?* are common.
- Knowing what other leaders and ministries are doing, and why, is valued.
- Multiple voices are encouraged to speak into issues.
- Risk taking and innovation are valued.
- The constant goal is maximum ministry results.
- Thinking gray is common.

Innovation comes from thinking differently. And this is a key requirement for leaders of deep influence: They take the time to think, probe, dialogue, mull, read, talk to others of deep influence, and always question what is, for the sake of what could be.

The downfall of many leaders is the crazy pace at which we run, which is why the issue of intentional living is so critical. Unless I build significant think time into my schedule, I don't have the time to question conventional wisdom and therefore I am unlikely to see significant breakthroughs in the ministry I lead. No one wants to repeat the same programs and activities over and over with the same mediocre results. Yet we do. Think time needs to be very high on our lists if we want to be people of deep influence.

Think time does not mean simply sitting still. For me, my best thinking comes when I am either writing or doing something deeply relaxing like fly fishing. In both cases, my mind clears of other issues, and I can focus in a relaxed way on issues that I have been considering. In the absence of other distractions I come to clarity and discover new ways in which our organization can be better at what it does. In fact, my annual weeks in Montana on vacation and fly fishing are some of the most productive weeks for ReachGlobal and for my writing.

The busier I am with activity, the less creative thinking I do. And while I may fool myself into thinking that all that activity is critical, the truth is that it takes only one significant breakthrough to change the whole equation and take us to a whole new level of ministry. But usually that breakthrough only comes when we have time to think. Activity is often the enemy of better ministry paradigms.

LEVERAGE

One of the reasons that some leaders develop deep influence is that they are always looking for ways to leverage their lives, opportunities, and ministries to greater advantage. This is a way of thinking. Leverage is the reason that I write books. I can reach far more people by writing than I can otherwise. I was so committed to gaining that leverage that I self-published my first two books when publishers said there was no market. The books were later picked up by a publisher.

In our discussion on intentional living I wrote about the importance of thinking through how we use our most valuable resource—our time. Wise individuals leverage their time for greatest ministry influence. When I travel, I often bring others with me, which exposes them to the world of missions and gives me time to develop a relationship. When I speak, whenever possible I also use the material I've developed for blogs or other writing projects. When traveling internationally, instead of traveling to many different locations I instead invite people to come to me at one location. It is all about maximizing opportunity for kingdom purposes.

In my fifties, I know that what I leave behind in others is more powerful than what I can accomplish myself. Thus, a great part of my time and energy today goes into mentoring and coaching others. My investment in their lives and ministries is leverage for me because their contribution multiplies my contribution.

Life should not be seen or lived as a series of random one-off events, but rather as interconnected ministry activities that, if thought through and wisely planned, can provide a critical mass of opportunity that allows us to leverage our time, gifting, and activity. Jesus was a master of this: By living life with His disciples, every event, conversation, or situation became an opportunity to grow them and, of course, in the power of the Holy Spirit they launched the church after His ascension.

Wise leaders also think leverage with respect to spending ministry dollars. Some of my ministry friends have a propensity to think very big when it comes to budgets for various initiatives. One of them asks my advice from time to time, and I tell him that I always divide his monetary needs by ten, and that is what he ought to be spending. Many ministry folks have never been in business where the bottom line means the difference between continued existence and closing the doors. They think God will provide, and rather than leveraging a reasonable amount to great effect, they try to raise far more than is actually needed.

Leaders of deep influence do not waste time, resources, opportunities, relationships, or strategy; they always look for ways to leverage these God-given resources for maximum ministry impact.

THE LENS OF LEADERSHIP

Great photographers are able to frame and capture images for which others would not have recognized the potential. They look through the lens with an eye to detail, color, and image placement; they possess an instinctive understanding of what will make for a great picture. Likewise, good leaders look at life through a highly nuanced leadership lens and see what others often do not see.

Individuals in ministry positions often look at their work

through overly optimistic eyes. They tend to see the wins and to extrapolate the conclusion that all is well. Just think about annual reviews that most people fill out or ministry reports that one reads. This is the airbrush approach: Celebrate the wins and airbrush out the problematic.

Many ministry leaders live in the airbrushed world. *After all*, they reason, *what we do is about God's work, so it is hard to measure progress.* In the ministry world we often put up with vague reports of progress without pressing into the specifics of what is really happening and how substantial the gains truly are. In addition, we often settle for far less than we could accomplish with honest scrutiny of the strategy, opportunity, and what could be, compared to what is.

This is why metrics of success are often missing in the ministry world. The very fact that we cannot define or measure success indicates that it is not high on our priority list. We would rather hope and assume that we are doing well than to actually measure and look reality in the face.

Wise leaders celebrate *wins* with those they lead. But they also look beyond the "good news" and evaluate the bigger picture, including problems and challenges that others may not want to see. Effective leaders are deeply realistic about what is *actually* taking place in the ministries they oversee. This is not a pessimistic view of life. Rather, it's the ability to honestly evaluate what the real picture is, the courage not to gloss over the negative, in order eventually to achieve even greater results.

Asking these kinds of questions is not always popular. Many staff feel that they are being critiqued and become defensive when asked probing questions. I have had senior staff become quite agitated at me for looking beneath the ministry hood to see where the rust and leaks are. Yet if leaders don't do that, who will? And it is not out of any unhappiness with staff, but out of a commitment to maximize the missional effectiveness to which God calls us.

As a photographer is able to frame a picture for maximum impact, good leaders are able to frame issues with their staff in ways that help them think strategically about their areas of responsibility. They ask questions that probe beneath the surface to help staff think about ways that ministry could be done more effectively, ways to leverage opportunity for greater impact.

In order for leaders to see the big picture, to be deeply realistic, and to frame the right issues, they must be people who take the time to think deeply about the ministry they lead and to ask the hard, uncomfortable questions that others don't want to ask.

Good leaders understand that their job is to affirm staff for the good news while also keeping staff from feeling comfortable. They keep pressing the missional agenda, asking the tough questions, reframing issues, and confronting reality.

The leadership lens is not an easy one to use. Those who use it, however, help their ministry maximize its impact and continually grow in effectiveness.

GAME CHANGERS

If you want to understand why some companies lack innovative ideas, think about the man who can't find his car keys.

His friend asks him why he's looking for the keys under the lamppost when he dropped them over on the lawn. "Because there's more light over here," the man explains.

For too many companies, that describes their search for new ideas, and it pretty much guarantees they won't go anywhere fast. While such a company can marginally improve what it's already good at, it misses out on the breakthroughs—those eureka moments when a new concept pops up, as if from nowhere, and changes a company's fortunes forever.

Those ideas, however, don't *really* come from nowhere. Instead they are typically at the edge of a company's radar screen, and sometimes a bit beyond. . . . In other words, they have to look away from the lamppost.

JOHN BESSANT, KATHRIN MÖSLEIN, AND BETTINA VON STAMM, "IN SEARCH OF INNOVATION," *THE WALL STREET JOURNAL*[1]

I could not agree more with this observation. I find that ministry organizations want to improve. But they are in large part so cautious about change or major new ideas that they tweak endlessly and see very little change in outcomes. Those who look away from the lamppost and are willing to take major risks in new ways of thinking are the ones who see the major rewards.

We have been looking away from the lamppost in ReachGlobal. For instance, instead of focusing our efforts on only partnering with other Free Church movements globally (the old way) or planting new Free Church movements (the old way), we now will partner with anyone who has the same theology, ethos, and missional goals, regardless of the denominational name over the door. That is a big shift, and it has opened up numerous partnerships for us with groups that are healthy, indigenous, self-supporting, interdependent, and reproducing. Rather than merely replicating *our* brand, we are now focusing on replicating Christ's bride.

We are no longer focused on what we can do by ourselves as missionaries (the old way). Now we focus on coming alongside other healthy movements and leaders, finding out what their needs are, and serving their needs, helping them to be as effective as possible in the planting of healthy churches. We are no longer in the driver's seat in many ways (the old way), but are now often the servants and assistants to others who are doing the driving.

All of that creates another seismic shift. Because we are serving others, we do not control anything, own anything, or count anything as "ours." That was the old way. The new way is giving ministry away freely, developing, empowering, and releasing others in meaningful, missional ministry. Interestingly, because we are no longer perceived to be controlling or owning, national partners are knocking on our door, asking if we can work with them. They know that we will serve them without having to be in charge.

Rather than relying on our expertise as American missionaries (the old way), we are actively inviting into our leadership ranks nationals from other cultures and nations, who bring with them expertise, knowledge, ideas, and insights we could never have imagined. Sure, it rocks the boat and causes waves at times, but we are far better off for taking the risk and allowing them to take us out of our comfort zone.

Tweaking our old ministry ideas by looking only under the lamppost will not give us the innovative ideas and leverage that are possible if we will take larger risks for greater rewards. Where are you looking?

Game changers are usually ways of thinking that are unconventional and have not been tried before. Indeed they are often deemed foolish or unworkable by others. Most people who lead look around and ask, What are others doing? Contrarian leaders look around and ask, What are others *not* doing that could be done to change the very nature of the game and therefore the outcome?

Every organization can find game changers if they think deeply enough. Leaders of deep influence are always looking for them because they want to maximize the influence of the organization rather than live with the status quo.

THINKING GRAY

Contrarian thinking often simply means that we think gray on issues until we must make a decision. It solicits as much input on a situation as possible, allowing the options to marinate in our minds, and doesn't make a final decision until it is necessary to do so. In the process, we often realize that there is an out-of-the-box solution that is far better than any of the proposed solutions. It is sometimes a creative combination of the best of the original options.

Some people think that quick decision making is a desirable skill, and they pride themselves on it. The truth is that a slow decision that has had significant input from a variety of sources usually is far better than a rapid one. Wise leaders always bring the best thinking to the table, including disparate viewpoints, refusing to settle for anything less than the very best solution.

Outside my office is another room that used to be occupied by my executive assistant. Today it has a table, four chairs, and whiteboards on two walls. I use that room far more than my office because this is the "think room" where, together with colleagues, I tackle complex issues in one of our many whiteboard sessions.

Out of those sessions have come all kinds of unique ideas and solutions that were far better than any one of us could have crafted. There is no such thing as an all-wise sage who invariably makes the right move. The sages of our day are those leaders who are secure enough to invite others to the table in order to find solutions that no one person could have found.

Having sought a variety of wise counsel, wise leaders will then mull on those ideas, always asking the question, "Is there an unconventional solution that would allow us to move forward in a leveraged way?" And they will often wait until the decision *must* be made to give themselves as much time as possible to consider alternatives. This is not decision avoidance. Gray thinking gives all of us the opportunity to continue to look for a new solution. Remember, conventional wisdom is always conventional, but it is rarely wisdom.

SIMPLIFYING COMPLEXITY

Remember the last strategic plan you crafted for your organization? How much of it was ever implemented? Can you remember the details of what you decided? And what about those things called *ministry philosophy*, *preferred future*, or *ministry outcomes*? Do you remember the wording of these for your organization? Are they helpful to you?

Consider this: Ministry is always complex. Complexity is confusing. Therefore complexity must be communicated with simplicity. Simplicity beats complexity every time!

Contrarian thinkers understand complexity, but they are always looking for ways to translate complex issues in simple ways that the organization can understand. Even the four basic questions every leader must ask for their ministry require a level of complexity: What is our mission? What are our guiding principles? What is our central ministry focus? What kind of culture do we need to intentionally create in order to fulfill our mission?

The problem with complexity is that it creates confusion, so some simply ignore it. Is it any wonder that mission drift takes place so easily?

Contrarian thinkers work hard to bring simplicity to complexity. Often they will use stories that grip the imagination and are memorable. Just think of the complex nature of grace and the ways in which we respond or don't respond to grace, and then think of the story of the prodigal son. So simple, so profound, so easily remembered!

Metaphors do the same thing. The baseball diamond used by purpose-driven churches takes complexity and simplifies it.[2] I lead from a sandbox, which takes complexity and simplifies it. A metaphor is something that can be easily understood and repeated. *And remembered*, which is the goal. With ReachGlobal's one-page picture of a sandbox we can communicate all the core commitments of a complex ministry organization. (For information on how to use the sandbox principle, see my book, *Leading from the Sandbox*.)

Sometimes just a phrase, intentionally and often repeated, does the trick. A friend of mine who pastors a large congregation tells the congregation, "We always must have a seat for the next person who is looking for a church home." He has said that for twenty-five years, and the church continues to grow. The value of always having a seat for the next individual has been owned by the congregation.

Leaders who can communicate complexity with simplicity are able to create an intentional organizational culture around those values that are most important. But simplifying complexity is a discipline that takes a great deal of thought, since complexity is just that—complex. But the time and effort is worthwhile. Simplicity forestalls confusion and provides an understandable, memorable vehicle by which people can live and communicate the ministry's mission.

THE DISCIPLINES OF THINKING AND DIALOGUE

It's worth repeating: People of deep influence are deep thinkers. Shallow thinking leads to shallow solutions and shallow results. Deep influence is a result of taking the time to deal with the issues of our inner lives, our relationship with God, our emotional intelligence, our shadow side, and many other internal disciplines and issues. None of this is possible without deep thinking.

Henri Nouwen wrote that we don't like to be silent and still because we are then confronted with the scaffolding of our lives, some of which we don't like, some of which we abhor.[3] Yet without taking the time to be silent and still we miss out on the ability to search deep things in our lives and in our ministries. There is a reason that the Lord says, "Be still, and know that I am God" (Psalm 46:10). It is in that stillness that we are confronted with His full majesty!

The contrarian thinking of people of deep influence is born out of a habitual discipline of extended periods of thinking. This is why I block off major portions of my year for thinking and writing, which often clarifies my thinking. I encourage pastors to develop a preaching team so that they can take time off from the weekly grind of preparation to stop and think deeply about their lives and ministries. If time to ponder and meditate deeply is important to us, then our schedules should reflect that practice. And think time should not be the first to go when other demands press into our schedules.

Equally important is time for deep dialogue with other leaders. It is not unusual for me to take twenty-four hours to be with another leader whom I respect and trust—including some international leaders—to share our lives and to talk through situations we face. This is thinking multiplied as two deep thinkers sharpen and challenge one another! Truly deep and contrarian thinkers are hard to find, but once found, they are treasured friendships to be nurtured and cultivated. They stretch me and I them.

PURSUING WISDOM

I have said that conventional wisdom is always conventional and rarely wisdom. One need only look at the life choices so many make to know that true wisdom is in short supply today. The book of Proverbs says that there is no greater gift than wisdom (see Proverbs 4), which starts with the fear of the Lord (see Proverbs 1:7) and then cascades down into our lives, relationships, priorities, and ministries. All of life is to be soaked in the wisdom from above (see James 3:13-18).

From a biblical perspective, wisdom is the ability to look at life situations and relationships from God's viewpoint and to respond in prudent ways that are consistent with His character. Wisdom takes into account potential solutions and unintended consequences, often by thinking gray. It then charts a course of action that is most likely to be productive and to minimize the unintended consequences.

Wisdom requires the pursuit of God, the pursuit of an understanding of ourselves, the counsel of others, and a willingness to go against the tide of conventional thinking. For men and women of deep influence, the pursuit of wisdom and the translation of wisdom into everyday situations is a top priority. A life of wisdom creates a powerful influence because it is a living out of the very wisdom of God.

Wise individuals think deeper, and they act more slowly and with more prudence and forethought than those who lack wisdom. Because of their measured responses they are more likely to act with both grace and truth. They are unthreatened by other strong opinions, and they invite those opinions to the table. They are also wise enough to know what they don't know and to listen carefully to others.

Effective leaders can also be decisive when they need to be. But as I have matured, I have learned that knee-jerk reactions to situations are usually more harmful than productive. I have learned to curb my anxiety when a situation cries out for attention *now*. I have learned that time is usually on my side, that trustworthy counselors will keep me from making foolish decisions, and that measured responses are far better than quick responses. In essence, I have grown in wisdom, and that growth has helped me lead better and has resulted in deeper influence.

I am a fan of the Wisdom Literature in Scripture. I am challenged by what is classified as "foolish" and drawn to the life of the "wise." I am reminded that truly wise individuals are contrarian thinkers in the eyes of the world. They go against the stream of common wisdom. I am also reminded that it is as I think deeply and biblically and heed the counsel of other wise individuals that I am at my best and avoid my worst. And finally, I am reminded of how far I have to go!

For Reflection and Discussion

1. On page 186 is a list of characteristics of a contrarian thinker. How do you evaluate your practices against these descriptors?

2. What game-changing strategies have you discovered in your organization? How did you discover them? How have they impacted what you do?

3. How do you practice "gray thinking"?

4. How do you simply communicate the complex philosophical underpinnings or strategies of what your ministry does?

5. How do you build in think and dialogue time so that you are able to find ways to leverage your resources to greater advantage?

CHAPTER TEN

LIVING WITH THE FREEDOM OF CLARITY

An outstanding trait of leaders of deep influence is that they enjoy significant clarity around things that are important to them. They know who they are, they understand what God has called them to be and do, and they are clear on the direction of the ministry or team they lead. They have learned the art of self-definition, and that self-definition is the compass that keeps them pointed in the right direction. They may think gray on many things, but on the most important topics there is no gray, only a self-defined clarity that provides the framework for their lives.

This clarity is sometimes mistaken as arrogance, which it is not. Arrogance comes from an attitude of pride and a lack of concern for others. Clarity comes from leaders paying attention to the hidden practices laid out in this book. It is the culmination of the practices we have studied thus far that gives us the gift of clarity in our lives.

Clarity brings us freedom in our personal lives and in our leadership. We can be unapologetic about God's call on our lives and the direction that we believe our organization needs to take. This comes not out of arrogance but from deep convictions and understanding that have been forged in our minds and souls over the years of following Him.

THE CLARITY OF KNOWING WHO GOD MADE *ME* TO BE

This is where the freedom of clarity begins: becoming comfortable with who God made me to be, as we explored in chapter 7. In my younger days I lived with a fair amount of anxiety, although I projected a fairly confident persona to the public. It was not so much about my strengths—I knew these well—but about believing that if my weaknesses became known I would not be a good leader.

What's humorous about that anxiety is that others already know our weaknesses, and our weaknesses are as much a part of God's intentional design as our strengths. I finally figured out in my forties that I could embrace the fact that God wired me with a few great strengths and that everything else could be put into the weakness category. Before I could be okay with God's wiring I had to embrace how God did *not* wire me.

How did this lead to freedom? I no longer had to pretend I was strong where I was not. I no longer had to have answers for questions I didn't fully understand. I no longer had to say yes to requests that were not in my areas of strength. And I no longer needed to worry about what others thought of all that because it was the God of the universe who sovereignly, uniquely, creatively made T. J. for a specific purpose, and because He chose not to gift me in any area that didn't fit that purpose.

People of deep influence live without pretense or guile. Who they are is what you get. Sure, we all have areas of life and character we are working on, but deep influencers manifest a consistency in our lives that attracts others. People know the *you* they can expect each day at work. They know the *me* they will encounter in a difficult meeting. They should see the same *you* and *me* in any other venue because we have no need for a mask, for lies about who we are.

Today I enjoy great personal freedom in being the best *me* that God created me to be, embracing His call on my life, accepting my strengths and weaknesses. Think about how that freedom and self-assurance can trickle down on those you lead. Secure leaders create secure teams.

THE CLARITY OF KNOWING WHAT GOD HAS CALLED *ME* TO DO

As we mature, we come to realize that there are roles in life that we do not want to play and are not gifted for. This narrows the field. This clarity comes from a deep understanding of our strengths, our God-given passions, and the formative streams that make up our life stories. (Remember the discussion we had around life themes in chapter 7.)

My own current role can be seen as a convergence between what I know about myself and the role I play. Along my career path I understood pieces of these, but it was not until I was in my late forties that I had all of them. Self-knowledge takes time and experimentation along the way. The good thing is that it is often in our fifties and sixties that we have the most significant influence, and a good part of that derives from clarity about what God has called us to do.

Knowing what God has called us to do is a freeing thing. That clarity allows us to say no to all kinds of opportunities; it grants us freedom to focus in on those opportunities that best fit God's macro call on our lives. The specifics may change, but the macro themes should become clearer and more focused as we move into our fifties and sixties.

This clarity is the compass we need both in our individual lives and in our organizational leadership role. People of deep influence do not aimlessly wander through life, allowing circumstances and other people to determine their direction. Rather, they have very deep convictions—an inner compass—about who God made them to be and what God has called them to do.

This may mean that we need to rethink how we structure our jobs and our priorities so that they line up with God's direction. Many pastors, for instance, assume that they should be generalists doing a shopping list of activities, when in fact they are really only designed for a limited number of tasks. Each person should focus his or her energies along the lane for which God has gifted him or her in order to achieve maximum effectiveness.

As an organizational leader I have carefully crafted my role, in dialogue with other ReachGlobal senior leaders, to maximize my effectiveness and to ensure that other leaders are playing to their strengths. Together we make a powerful team because we have individual and team clarity on what God has gifted and called us to do. Periodically we reevaluate to ensure that each one is in his or her lane.

THE CLARITY OF BEING COMFORTABLE IN MY OWN SKIN

The self-assurance that comes with being comfortable in our own skin is a huge gift when we achieve it. For me it took many years. This is a combination of understanding ourselves, our strengths and shadow sides, and the lanes we were made to run in. It is living with a divine okay that we are who we are and that we are not what we are not—and never will be, and that too is okay. It is the place where we no longer have anything to prove or lose, a place of freedom.

Getting comfortable in one's own skin takes time and intentionality. For me it took time to learn to enjoy being an introvert in an extrovert job, and today it fits me well. It took time to learn that I didn't have to have the answers to all problems, or to live with anxiety when crises hit. It took time to learn to trust my instincts.

Learning to live with a nothing-to-prove-nothing-to-lose attitude lifts all kinds of weight from our shoulders. Choosing to be transparent rather than holding our cards close to our vest allows others to understand us. Learning how to be self-defining, honest, and upfront, while still staying connected to those who might disagree with us, keeps us in relationship.

A test of one's comfortableness in one's own skin is his or her acceptance of the fact that not everyone likes the version of himself or herself that God made. Now, if most of those we lead have serious problems with us, we need to look carefully at ourselves. But even when we're leading well, a few will dislike us or our style, and those few may be very vocal in their opinions.

This is where leading through team is so important. I have many deficits, but the better my team is, the less those deficits impact the organization as a whole. If someone in the organization does not like my leadership style, he or she can certainly find someone on the team with whom he or she resonates.

Growing our emotional health is important. Those who are comfortable in their own skin are so either because of deep arrogance ("I am right, so I don't have to worry about what others think") or because they are deeply cognizant of who they are and are sensitive to the needs of others. The former, arrogant type of "comfortableness" is damaging to those around the leaders. The latter is a comfortableness of self-understanding, understanding of calling, and deep humility that allows people to lead from God-given identity and with great sensitivity to those around them.

Humility is central to this equation. Pride is concerned about how others see us, about being right, about managing our reputation and image. Humility is knowing that we have nothing to prove and nothing to lose, that we don't need to manage our reputation, and that we are simply broken vessels (the apostle Paul's words in 2 Corinthians 4), whom God uses for His purposes.

People are drawn to transparency, not a managed image or spin. People see through the latter, but the former engenders deep influence.

THE CLARITY OF SAYING NO
AND FEELING GOOD ABOUT IT

Living with clarity is all about understanding God's calling on us and on the team or organization we lead. By definition that means we also live with clarity about what God has *not* called us to do. Yet the activity of our lives, the expectations of others, and the opportunities that come to people of influence all conspire to take clarity and turn it into functional ambiguity. A test of our clarity is our ability to say no to anything that doesn't fulfill God's calling—often—and feel good about it afterward!

Yes and *no* define what is important to us, what we are called to, and how we will invest our time. As a young leader I was more driven by *yes* than by *no*, both because I wanted to please those I led and because I did not have the focused clarity I have today.

This is equally true on an organizational level. Every

organization has a mission that defines it; hopefully it also has guiding principles, a central ministry focus, and a culture that it is intentionally creating. That clarity of focus can easily be subverted by trying to be everything to everyone. Leaders spend a great amount of time and attention to bringing maximum clarity to the organization they lead, and then keeping that clarity in front of everyone all the time.

Whether personally or organizationally, the central reality is: *A no is really a yes.* In saying no to many things, we say yes to the specific call of God on our lives or on our ministries. Following the call of God is an ongoing series of yes-and-no choices that keeps us in the lane in which He has called us to run. Seen in that light, both *yes* and *no* are positive words, and they represent intentional choices that allow us to fulfill God's personalized call on our lives.

THE CLARITY OF A CAUSE WORTH GIVING MY LIFE TO

How passionate are you about the work to which God has called you? Is it something that gets you up in the morning, ready to tackle the day, knowing that it is worth your life? That is one of the secrets of people of deep influence. *They believe with all their hearts that what they do matters, that it is of eternal consequence, and that every day counts in their journey.*

I believe in the cause God has given our organization: "We are a gospel-centered movement changing lives, communities, and institutions worldwide in the power of God's

Spirit." Even more significant for me, God's call on our ministry aligns with God's call on my life and with my convictions, so the organization's mission and my personal mission converge quite nicely. And every day of my life is a day to advance the organization's cause.

The absence of a compelling cause in one's personal and work life is a debilitating condition that sucks away energy, diminishes joy, and compromises impact. Too many people suffer from the condition. This is especially sad in light of the fact that God has created each of us specifically to accomplish something of great value for Him and then gifted each one for that specific influence (see Ephesians 2:10). The route to deep influence is in understanding His calling and finding a cause congruent with that calling that fuels our individual passion, conviction, joy, and eternal impact.

These words may frustrate you because, unlike me, you may not be in a position of leadership. And those of you who are have not articulated a cause worth giving your life to. You are not alone. And there is hope!

A cause worthy of our lives starts with us. We are not dependent on others to determine God's call on our lives. That is our responsibility! Once we know what that call is and how He has wired us, we live out that calling no matter where we are. This is particularly important for those who don't yet have convergence between the strengths and passions God has implanted in them and their day-to-day work. We can live out His call vocationally or avocationally. The importance is that we are living it out. If it is truly His call and our passion, we will find ways to answer that call no matter what we are doing vocationally!

Many people of deep influence live their lives in the secular workplace, where they live out God's call on their lives. They know that full-time ministry is not the only way to impact our world, and in fact those who are in vocational ministry will often never touch the people and institutions they can touch. They are the Nehemiahs and Daniels and Esthers who have amazing influence because of their character and commitment to bring the ethics of the kingdom to the marketplace.

The fact is that entire organizations can be influenced and transformed when God's people live out their cause in the marketplace. People are treated better, ethics are higher, excellence grows, and communities are made better because people of deep influence quietly fulfill their cause and God's call on their lives.

If you are a part of a Christian organization, never underestimate your influence on the organization in helping them come to clarity regarding their cause. Most leaders who don't have a clearly defined cause would love to have one but need help getting there. Leadership can come from the bottom, the middle, or the top if done wisely but persistently.

For years at the EFCA national office, I did not have a senior position, but through my writing, my relationships, and the team I led I was able to have influence on the direction of our movement. In fact, position is not the key factor—influence is. Figure out how you can have influence, and encourage missional clarity and a life-worthy cause from whatever place you occupy in the organization.

There are times when it is worth looking for a different ministry organization to serve. This may be appropriate if you are convinced that your organization cannot come to clarity around a passionate cause, or that you will not find convergence between your strengths, wiring, and call in your current work. Some organizations simply lack the will to live out a clear and passionate cause because it is far more comfortable to settle for what is, rather than to press into what could and should be. I would not last very long in such a "comfortable" organization, and neither would most people of deep influence.

The very fact that you are willing to look elsewhere may be a wake-up call to your organization that not all is well. If it is not, it is confirmation that you are making the right choice! The world has far too many sleepy and nonmissional congregations and ministries. Deep influence is rarely found there.

I am so passionate about the cause of which I am a part that I have told my family that if anything ever happens to me in the pursuit of that cause, they should know that I left this earth a happy and fulfilled man. The cause of the gospel is worth everything to me. The multiplication of gospel-centered churches that bring hope to the hopeless and transformation to communities is worth every bit of energy I expend, and even my life. For all of us, the gospel is a cause that is God-sized, eternity-driven, and worth the prize that Paul spoke of.

People of deep influence are driven by a cause greater than themselves and one that has eternal consequences. They are driven by the same passion that drove Jesus to take the hard road to Gethsemane. They never settle for a life of comfort over a life of influence and impact, and if it comes to it, they are willing to pay any price for the object of their passion.

Do you have such a cause?

THE CLARITY OF DEALING WITH UNFINISHED BUSINESS

On December 4, 2007, I went to the emergency room because of severe breathing difficulties. What followed was a forty-three-day hospital stay, thirty-five of them in the ICU hovering between life and death. It is only by God's grace and mercy that I survived against impossible medical odds. I was fifty-one years old at the time. It is sobering to me that I never should have woken up from my drug-induced coma or seen my fifty-second birthday.

None of us knows how many days are allotted to us except God, who wrote each one of them in His book long before we were born (see Psalm 139:16). What we do know is that God gives us the time we need to fulfill His assignment for us on this earth, just as He did for Jesus (see John 17:4). This is why intentional living is so important. We want to live at the intersection of His call and His gifting for His purposes.

Living with clarity is living with the recognition that life is a gift, each day is a day of grace, and life's duration is uncertain. Therefore we want to live with as little unfinished business in our lives as possible. There is great freedom in that because unfinished business is like carrying rocks in our backpacks—burdens that weigh on our consciences. Those burdens can be areas of our lives that we have not completely given to God, relationships that are broken and need reconciliation, things that God has been nudging us about but to which we have not responded.

People of deep influence are intentional about living with as little unfinished business as possible. To the extent that it depends on them, they do what they can to live in the freedom of a clear conscience before God and others.

Periodically I ask myself what unfinished business remains in my life. Usually I find some, since God continually reveals to me new areas where I need to press into Him or pursue a higher level of obedience. We will never be free from all unfinished business until we see Him face to face. But continual progress toward closing that gap is freedom.

A critical area for unfinished business is in the area of relationships. This side of heaven, we will never be free from conflict in relationships. The apostle Paul had people who intentionally hurt his ministry (see Philippians 1:15-18). He also had a relational breakdown with Barnabas, who had mentored and encouraged him, over another relational breakdown with John Mark (see Acts 15:36-40). Jesus had his detractors in the Pharisees (see Matthew 16:1-12). And in our ministry settings there will always be people who disagree with a leader's direction, or who simply don't like him or her. It is one of the inevitable burdens of leadership.

People of deep influence understand this. But they are also men and women of peace who are always willing—to the extent that they can—to foster relational peace and understanding. They will go the second and third mile to resolve what can be resolved, and then live at peace with what cannot be resolved.

This is not an easy discipline. It means that when others fight dirty with us, we don't respond with their tactics; we are called to be "as shrewd as snakes and as innocent as doves" (Matthew 10:16). Sometimes living at peace means that we live with the pain that others inflict, and we leave our reputations in God's hands. Sometimes it means that we agree to disagree, but refuse to fight, slander, or impugn those who may inflict the same on us. Sometimes it means sitting down and listening carefully, trying to understand another's point of view, even if we do not agree with it.

This is not about accepting unbiblical behavior, which so often occurs in the church or Christian organizations behind a masquerade of spiritual rhetoric. It does mean that we do not respond in the *spirit* that others may display toward us, and that to the extent that we can, we will live at peace with all people (see Romans 12:18). Where we need to confront, we will do so with honesty, but also with the desire for understanding and reconciliation. When that is not possible, we may have to take action as leaders, but we remain committed to displaying godly character and not sinning in our anger or pain (see Galatians 6:1-2).

The test of our character is not when all is going well, but when we are under attack. That is when the God-instilled qualities built into our core being become evident. People of deep influence are slow to anger, are willing to confront in love, always desire understanding and reconciliation, are wise and measured in their response to attack, refuse to adopt the tactics of revenge, and leave their reputations in the hands of God.

This question of our reputations is perhaps one of the hardest lessons to learn. I have had periods when my reputation was dragged through the mud by those who despised me. (I don't know of any good leader who has never had this happen.) Everything in me wanted to fight back, to set the record straight, to get even with those who had inflicted deep pain.

A valuable lesson I learned from David in Psalms 37 and 73 is that at the end of the day, God is able to defend my reputation far better than I ever can. And when I try, I end up adopting the very tactics that I found repugnant. What God wanted of me was to live with His character, in the power of His Spirit, and let Him, in His (usually) gentle manner, deal with those who hurt me. It was in these times that I learned the most valuable lessons of character and leadership.

THE CLARITY OF ACCOUNTABILITY

All people of deep influence have learned to live under accountability. They are not free agents but individuals who have learned to follow, and who welcome the accountability under which they work and lead.

Many would-be leaders have not learned to follow and therefore do not deserve to be followed. Whether they are senior pastors who don't believe they need to listen to their board, staff to their supervisors, or missionaries to their team or mission leaders, there are too many people who believe they are free agents in the ministry world. For many it would be a shock to actually work in the nonministry world, where standards of accountability are often far higher and where free agency is rarely tolerated.

Accountability is a necessity. If we work under individuals to whom we are unwilling to answer, we need to find someone to whom we will be. Living with a lack of accountability is dangerous—for anyone.

Followership is a crucial prelude to leadership, and the higher the level of leadership, the more accountability there ought to be, because the stakes are higher. In our organization, one of the first questions we ask about someone being considered for leadership is, has he or she followed well?

The inability to follow well has its roots in a rebellious spirit and usually translates into one's unwillingness to follow God, not only human leadership. A rebellious spirit was at the root of King Saul's flawed character, which led God to anoint a new king for Israel—one who had a heart after God's (see 1 Samuel 13:14). At its core a rebellious spirit is about going our own way, which is the classic definition of sin in Isaiah 53:6.

I am blessed to work for a highly empowering leader who allows me to play to my strengths, who avoids micromanaging, and who is supportive. But he is so because he trusts me to be sensitive to his leadership and the direction of the EFCA as a whole. He knows that after robust dialogue, either with him or with the EFCA leadership team, I will always play ball—even when I, left on my own, would have done differently. He also knows that I will never undermine him or the senior team in words, actions, or attitudes. The moment I do that, I will have lost my moral authority to lead under him.

With that blessing comes a huge responsibility both to my supervisor and to the One to whom I am ultimately accountable. Responsibility to lead my life well, since who I am spills over to others. Responsibility to bring clarity to the organization I lead, since that clarity impacts everyone and everything we do. Responsibility to develop, empower, and release individuals for maximum effectiveness. And responsibility to create an ethos and culture in ReachGlobal that is healthy and productive.

Accountable leaders model a biblical truth for everyone in the organization: We all live under authority. In fact, as part of my own example to 550 staff members, I annually publish my own key result areas and annual ministry plan. In doing so, I send a strong signal that I am willing to be held accountable to myself, to my supervisor, and to my organization. I would do this even if Bill did not ask me for an annual plan. I choose to live under authority, and my response to my earthly authority is a reflection of my response to my heavenly authority.

LIVING WITH FREEDOM

People of deep influence live remarkably free from anxiety and fear. In knowing what God has—and has *not*—called them to, in being comfortable in their own skin, in pursuing a passionate cause, and in living with little unfinished business, they are free to live with confidence, energy, and direction.

This freedom is a gift, and it is one of the magnets that draws people to deep influencers. Most of the world lives with high degrees of fear and anxiety rather than freedom and joy. Living with clarity is really about living in the center of God's will for our lives. And the closer to the center we live, the greater freedom we enjoy. It is a place where we can trust Him to be our advocate, to guard our reputation, to empower our lives, and to direct our future.

It should be clear that in the end we serve an audience of One. This was the secret to Paul's confidence and joy in the midst of difficult circumstances and people. He knew that ultimately he would give an account to his Lord. He lived with great clarity and a clean conscience, and he understood that many of the problems he faced were mere distractions to serving Christ. Such clarity is the greatest freedom of all.

For Reflection and Discussion

1. In which area discussed in this chapter do you feel you need greater clarity? How will you get there?

2. How does your clarity in these areas impact your day-to-day life and leadership?

3. In what ways does your clarity contribute to your personal and professional freedom?

CHAPTER ELEVEN

POWERFUL TRANSPARENCY

What is the secret that draws people to us, or us to others? Certainly it includes the qualities that we have examined in this book, all of which contribute to deep influence. It is not just one quality or practice, but confluences of practices that matter. One of these is the practice of transparency, by which others are invited into your life in authentic ways that allow the real you to rub off on others.

I am by nature a fairly private person who thinks before I talk, usually responds in a measured way, and is not overly verbal. Over the years, however, I have chosen to become far more transparent to others than I once was. This has been an intentional shift based on my conviction that transparency with others is a powerful tool, not only in the development of deeper relationships, but in developing deep influence.

The most powerful influence is that of life on life, where who *we* are rubs off on others, influencing who *they* become. The guiding factor in that transaction is the ability of the others to know and understand us. Without providing the opportunity to see into our hearts, minds, priorities, and relationships, our inner persons remain hidden and mysterious to others. They may see something they like and respect, but what lies behind the image they see remains opaque and hidden.

Opening our lives to others is much like opening our homes. It is an invitation to come in, make themselves at home, and commune as friends do. I may think I know someone well, but actually being in his or her home changes the equation because I see family interactions, the contents of bookshelves, and all kinds of interesting things that I would never know without being in that home.

The same is true with our lives. Opening our lives to others lets them into the genuine inner person. When we do so, whatever God is doing in the transformation of our lives becomes a point of connection in the lives of others—for us and for God, and therefore for influence.

It is really quite amazing how open Paul was in his letters, the New Testament Epistles. He shared his failures as well as his successes, and one is often able to read his emotions as he writes.

For instance, disclosing a thorn in the flesh that God chose not to remove is a pretty personal piece of information, especially when he explains that it was to keep him humble and dependent (see 2 Corinthians 12:7-10). He was not afraid to share his spiritual journey, including his being caught up in the third heaven where he received a glimpse of God (see 12:2). And he was open about the pain of opposition from fellow Christians who tried to build their ministry by hurting his (see Philippians 1:15-18).

His goal of finishing the race well and his desire for intimacy with Christ are laid out for all to see. The spiritual lessons he had learned along the way are shared as an encouragement for us—lessons like contentment with little or with much (see Philippians 4:11-13). He learned this truth in the real life he lived and freely shared it with us.

We often read Paul's letters in a theological manner. And with reason, as Paul was the consummate theologian of the New Testament. But try reading them as letters of self-disclosure, in which Paul intentionally and openly shared his life, emotions, dreams, struggles, and even failures, and you see a person like you and me, straining to live out the call of God, becoming the man of God and embracing the power of God—exposing his tears, disappointments, and joys. Think of how dry his writing would have been if it were simply theological truths devoid of real-life struggles or emotion.

How true this was of David in the Psalms, where he shared his heart so openly that sometimes we don't know what to make of it (as with the imprecatory psalms). The very reason we run to the Psalms in times of difficulty is that we find God's presence there in the middle of real-life challenges.

Even the God of the universe, throughout the Old Testament, chose to reveal His love, anger, frustration, joy, or sorrow over the people of Israel. Over and over in the prophets He opens His very heart to us so that we glimpse not only His holiness but the range of emotions behind His love. We see this in the life of Christ in the Gospels, where a real man (and real God) was disclosing Himself in a way that we would never expect of God.

It is in that self-disclosure of Paul or God that we are able to relate, to understand, and to be challenged to respond. Their self-disclosure becomes a magnet to draw us to them, to hear what they have to say, and to do something. Their transparency draws us into their hearts, minds, and message.

Of course the most amazing self-disclosure came in the form of the Incarnation, when God broke into history in the person of Jesus Christ so that we could know and understand God. As Jesus has called us to the same ministry that He performed (see John 17:18), it follows naturally that we should make the same effort to live transparently with others and make our lives accessible to them. Then we, like Jesus, have an amazing opportunity to influence others for Christ. He disclosed God to us through His life. We disclose Jesus to others through our lives.

LACK OF TRANSPARENCY

There are a number of reasons that we choose not to be as self-disclosing as we could be. Perhaps the most common reason is that our pride prevents us from sharing lessons or situations in which we have proven less than we should be or really messed up. It is pride that causes Christ-followers to wear false masks, pretending that all is well when in fact they are struggling with significant difficulties and failures.

This is unfortunate because our lack of transparency often prevents others from understanding us, learning from us, and being influenced by our lives. Hiding ourselves is not necessary if we are comfortable with who we are, how God made us, and the fact that we are merely cracked pots whom God graciously uses for His purposes.

There are churches that I love to attend because they demonstrate a transparency among the people that is different from the norm. The people are quick to strike up conversations and are equally willing to freely share their stories of how they came to faith. There is no pretense or mask. They talk about failed marriages, struggles with pornography, affairs, bankruptcies, issues with pride, relational breakdowns . . . and how God has redeemed them.

The lack of transparency among so many of us is a tactic intended to preserve our dignity, but in reality it hurts the very objective that we want most—spiritual influence. The reason that we go to the Psalms in times of difficulty is that we want honest faith, not a fake faith. The reason we attract people when we are transparent is the same—people can relate to honest faith, real life, and humanly irreparable situations, but not fake faith. Thus the more transparent we are in our own lives and the more real we are to those around us, the more influence we can have.

As a general rule, pride hides the true inner person in order to present an image that is better than we are. Humility (nothing to prove, nothing to lose) seeks to be who we are all the time, genuine versions of us. It is the real person, rather than the false front, that will most powerfully influence the lives of others. People cannot relate to false personas (and usually see through them), but they can relate to real people. Further, simply being who we are means that we don't need to manage a public self and a private self—a complicated dual persona. Just being me in the process of God's transformation is a comfortable and honest place to live.

Since there will not be a perfect me till I see Jesus, I don't have to pretend that there is a perfect me now. Acknowledging the imperfect me gives me the freedom to admit failure or sin or mistakes when they occur and simply say, "I am sorry. Will you forgive me?" Those powerful words, too seldom used, bring great respect, and the lack of them brings relational breakdown that can last for decades.

Pride, the nemesis of leaders, often keeps us from admitting our fault, and in the effort to look good we end up hurting others and losing influence. Pride is the antithesis of a transparent life.

Another reason for lack of transparency is fear—fear that we will not look good, fear that others may not like us if they knew the real us, and fear that others might use our information against us. On this last point, we clearly need to be wise in terms of what we disclose to whom. The rule is that the level of disclosure goes up as relational trust grows, and we never simply disclose everything to everyone.

Think, though, about messages you have heard that resonated with you. Are they simply good theology, or are they also the disclosure of how the one preaching has personally wrestled with the theology? Truth without application is not very helpful. The application is where we best touch and understand the text itself. When I use my own struggles, funny or not, to illustrate the truth, I invite in others who can relate to my story.

Transparency is really about authenticity. It is living with a commitment to be *who we are* with *whomever we are with* all the time. It is living without masks or facades.

It is also about an unselfish life in which we make the effort to invite others in, knowing that we pay a price for that: our time and energy. Selfishness says, Leave me alone. It is easier that way. Selflessness says, I care about you and am willing to open my life to you.

THE AUTHENTIC SELF

In a previous chapter we looked at the freedom of being who God made us to be and being comfortable in our own skin. This comfortableness allows us to increasingly set aside the need for pretense that we are something we are not, and it gives us the freedom to confidently disclose who we are.

Authentic people have authentic issues in their marriages, families, work, and other relationships. They have fear and anxiety, become defensive when certain buttons are pushed, and suffer from insecurities. This side of heaven, we are plagued with all kinds of challenges that relate to our emotional intelligence, wiring, weaknesses, shadow side, and vulnerabilities. Anyone who pretends otherwise is either fooling himself or herself or living with false pretenses.

What people need from leaders of deep influence is honesty, appropriate to the situation, about issues they face and how they deal with them. I do not look like an insecure person, and generally I am not. But when I share some of my insecurities with groups of leaders, they sit up and listen. They are surprised. But guess what? They also relate. I am not the only one with insecurities, and in disclosing my struggles I am more likely to be heard and encourage others.

Our transparency with others creates an atmosphere of transparency in which it becomes safe to talk about those issues that plague us all but that we are afraid to disclose. Creating that atmosphere is a gift to the team you lead and the people you influence because, hidden and unresolved, these issues hurt us. Through self-disclosure we create a culture of authenticity where struggles are acknowledged, people are encouraged, and facades are discouraged. It is a culture of authentic grace and truth.

This combination of grace and truth that characterized Christ is crucial to healthy transparency (see John 1:14). Being truthful means that we are committed to walking in truth, speaking truth, and creating cultures of truth. But truth must always be merged with grace if it is not going to be harsh and hard. And it starts with us adopting an honest, nondefensive manner that does not blame or throw stones but simply lives and speaks truth graciously as a way of life.

An example of authenticity and honesty carries over to organizational culture as well. I am familiar with many churches and Christian organizations where there is more airbrushed gloss than truth about what is really happening in the ministry. Problems are ignored or spiritualized, problem people are not dealt with, and ministry effectiveness—or lack of it—is not honestly examined. It is always interesting to see a more authentic leader come into such situations and actually name things for what they are! It is a refreshing change for those who don't like the facade and a threatening change for those who do. Many Christian organizations are just waiting for such a leader who is transparent about his or her personal challenges and the challenges of the ministry he or she leads.

My honesty elicits honesty among others, and it is transparent, honest discussion that allows an organization to draw out the best rather than hide the worst. If you are not naturally very self-disclosing, I encourage you to take some small, intentional steps toward greater transparency. You will be surprised at the power of those small steps in others' responses to you and the impact on the group you work with. It will encourage you to continue to increase your personal level of self-disclosure.

Authentic self-disclosure is a significant element in developing trust with others and within an organization. Trust is based on understanding the thinking of leaders, minimizing surprises where possible, and providing venues for dialogue around important issues. That starts with the self-disclosure of a leader who is willing to put his or her cards on the table and then invite dialogue. Secretive leaders engender mistrust, while self-disclosing leaders build high trust.

Another ministry-changing venue for transparency is with schedules and work. Ministry roles, particularly in the church or in mission work, can often be unstructured (not a good thing) and lacking accountability. Two consequences of this are, first, a lack of intentionality in schedules and work goals, and second, a lack of trust in leaders who live unreliably, by the seat of their pants.

Picture a pastor who makes his or her schedule on the run, does not keep his or her staff up to speed on his or her priorities or schedule, and changes direction on a whim. I have consulted in situations like these, and the common complaint is, "We don't know what he does." That is a dangerous way for a leader to live and lead because behind that observation is a trust issue. Lack of information breeds mistrust because lack of accountability breeds mistrust.

All senior leaders in our organization make their online calendars available to one another, which means that information is available on what each one is up to. In addition, most months I publish my schedule to my prayer team so they can be praying through the month. My point is that transparency in all areas of life is healthy; it models openness, it shuns dangerous secretiveness, and it supports a life of ongoing accountability. Transparency and accountability go hand in hand.

Transparency also applies to ministry results. There is a significant tendency—perhaps even pressure—to speak in inflated terms about what God is actually doing in our ministries. Truth and honesty are high priorities for people of deep influence. They are willing to share about disappointing results. Dishonesty about ministry results is incompatible with the God of truth. And since ministry fruit is ultimately His responsibility, we can simply serve faithfully and leave those results up to Him.

Honesty, transparency, accountability, and a life of truth all engender trust and model healthy life practices. Those practices also keep our lives in safe waters and contribute to lives of deep influence.

SPIRITUAL TRANSFORMATION REDUX

In chapter 4 we discussed the goal that Jesus has for our lives, which is to make each person into the best version of himself or herself that is possible through the work of His Spirit. This process is the spiritual transformation of our hearts, our minds, our priorities, and our relationships.

Remember, perfection is not the goal of our lives—we will achieve that only when we see Him face-to-face. Paul challenges us to only live up to the level of maturity that we have already reached (see Philippians 3:16). The most powerful indicator of God's supernatural work in our lives is this transformation because it is only possible through God's work. It is as people see those changes and want the same for their lives that they press into how and why we have changed. Or are quietly influenced to move in the same direction themselves.

This transformation is a powerful contributor to our deep influence with others as they see God's work in our lives. I am a gentler, kinder, more empathetic person than I was twenty years ago. Those who have known me over that time can see the change, and it is a testimony to God's work in my life. It gives me greater influence, and it becomes an encouragement to those who need to experience that same transformation themselves.

Paul made this point to Timothy when he wrote, "Be diligent in these matters; give yourself wholly to them, so that everyone may see your progress. Watch your life and doctrine closely. Persevere in them, because if you do, you will save both yourself and your hearers" (1 Timothy 4:15-16). It was precisely Timothy's growth that would be an encouragement to those who knew him and would give him credibility in his ministry.

Never allow anyone to place you on a pedestal, as if you have arrived. That is a dangerous and dishonest place to be. Rather, be disclosing about where God is working in your life as a reminder to others that the work of God's Spirit is central to our lives and that all of us are on the journey. We cannot influence others from a pedestal; we don't really occupy it, and no one can realistically follow us to it. We can influence others as we are transparent about our own spiritual journey and the lessons we are learning.

Think through your circle of friends and acquaintances

and ask yourself the question, How transparent am I with them? I have found that the more transparent I am in my leadership role, the more those I lead appreciate and respect me. Just being me—as long as I am engaged in God's transformation—is far more powerful than maintaining a persona of me.

One powerful area of regular transparency is sharing what God is showing us as we pursue Him. That openness is an encouragement to others to also be pressing into their relationship with God and to avoid the trap of being so busy serving Him that we are not cultivating our relationship with Him.

The power of a group of individuals regularly sharing their cutting edge issues with God is truly significant. It is leverage in the lives of all present because we are exposed to many lessons being learned. It is leaders who set the culture for this kind of sharing. To the extent that we are open and transparent, others will be as well.

PRESENCE

Our greatest influence will come through our personal interactions with others. Distant and unapproachable leaders may look impressive for a while, but they will not have the kind of deep influence that a present and approachable leader has. Our greatest influence is life on life, and that requires relationship—time with others sharing work or life.

People who want to have deep influence love people and are willing to invest in them. While I am by nature more of an introvert than an extrovert, much of my life is spent with key individuals who are my colleagues and whom I desire to influence. My writing is merely an extension of that time with people, where the real lessons are learned and the deepest influence takes place. This is where the power of transparency is at its best.

Since high school I have practiced the discipline of spending quality time with a select number of individuals—usually around ten at any given time—and continue to do so to this day. These may be formal mentoring relationships or often informal, where time together and dialogue allow life-on-life influence. Sometimes it is fairly one-way, sometimes two-way. These are individuals of all ages whom I believe God desires me to influence for a season.

One of the mistakes in the Western world, as it relates to spiritual transformation, is to focus on classroom teaching or reading. While these can be valuable pieces of the equation, the reality is that the most powerful growth and transformation is life-on-life, rather than primarily classroom. That is why Jesus lived with twelve disciples, dialogued with them, did ministry with them, and even sent them on their own for special ministry. His presence was a powerful positive influence.

At fifty-seven years old I know that my deepest influence will come through a new generation of leaders whom I can have a part in developing. These are national leaders from around the world, as well as those from this country. This has become one of my five core priorities, and it takes place first through personal presence, by which I invite them into my life. Once I've established presence and a relationship, we can continue mentoring face-to-face or from a distance.

What is interesting about presence is that we don't know how God is going to rub off on others. Often people will say to me, "Do you know what I remember about our time together?" They then relate some facet of a conversation that I don't even remember. The Holy Spirit had been working just where they needed encouragement or a specific word, and I had no clue at the time. But that is the magic of life-on-life interaction.

Because time is precious, I think and pray about whom I choose to invest in personally through my presence. I want to develop other deep-influence individuals, who will in turn do the same. At its heart this is about transparency and inviting others into my life.

TRANSPARENCY IN FAILURE AND PAIN

Our world celebrates success and denigrates failure (unless you are a Hollywood celebrity and fail spectacularly, in which case you are now a smashing success by some twist of logic). But the truth is that we learn the most valuable lessons through failure, not success, and our transparency about our failures and pain is perhaps far more important than teaching people of our successes. In failure the best lessons are learned, the best faith is forged, and the best transformation takes place. So why would we hide our failures?

One's willingness to share his or her whole story, where

appropriate, becomes a powerful encouragement to others who are often struggling with the same issues or believe that, because they have "failed," God cannot use them. The fact is that many disappointments that we view as failures are not really failures at all but are so only in our own minds. Older leaders would do younger leaders a great favor if they would share their own stories more transparently. Often young leaders view their elders as having sailed through life with a minimum of pain and failure. Usually just the opposite is true.

My perspective on hard times is very different today than it was when I was a young leader. I understand success and failure differently, have the perspective of time to see how God used pain for my benefit, and have seen His faithfulness in what looked like impossible situations. Not only did I not know all of those things as a young leader going through hard times, but the advice I received then was not very helpful: God will work it all out! God did, but not in the way well-intentioned people meant. One of the realities is that some things don't get worked out this side of heaven—no matter how hard one prays or how hard one tries.

God does not always fix broken situations. But He is always faithful in the process when we choose to press into Him. Faithfulness does not mean that God intervenes to fix all situations but that He is faithful to us in the middle of brokenness. I wish I had understood that as a young leader. I willingly share my experiences today to encourage the next generation of leaders who are walking through their own broken places.

Success is not living without pain or tough times. Nor is it necessarily seeing spectacular ministry results; often the results will be dismal from our point of view. Success is faithfully living at the intersection of God's gifting and His calling on our lives, wherever that should be. Deep influence is not dependent on achieving success or acclaim by our peers' standards, but on cultivating the hidden practices we have been studying, which mold a strong, deep core of spiritual strength and resolve that guides all that we do and everything that we are.

All of us have paid our share of "dumb tax"—things that we would not do again and lessons learned the hard way. Our willingness to share our dumb tax with others can save them the pain of learning it themselves. I often ask leaders to divulge their past stupidity for my own benefit, and I encourage leaders to regularly share dumb tax with one another.

I am always amazed at the response from young and old leaders alike when I speak on pain, suffering, and brokenness from a biblical and personal perspective. I have had more than my share of difficult times, including debilitating physical illness. People thank me over and over for sharing transparently. They are hungry for a perspective on their own situations and struggles, and they're encouraged that they are not alone.

Each of us who is faithful is simply one more in the line of heroes named in Hebrews 11, who lived by faith even when the chips were down. There is power in stories of brokenness transformed by grace!

STAYING TRANSPARENT WITH OURSELVES

A life of transparency with others has the benefit of encouraging us to be transparent with God about our lives as well. Certainly God is fully aware of our struggles. He does not need our transparency, but we do. Not for the purpose of guilt but as a matter of knowing where He is gently—sometimes not so gently—prodding us to move closer to Him and away from the distractions of self and sin.

Understanding our own hearts, our particular vulnerabilities, our shadow side, and areas where we need to grow spiritually keeps us from pride, from self-satisfaction, from the often unbiblical view of life and success. This humbling practice keeps us grounded in our need of God's grace and presence. All of us would like to think that we are better than we are, more mature than we are, and less vulnerable than we are. When we measure our lives against the truth of God's Word, we realize that none of that is true. We need God desperately and one another deeply. Our hearts, by themselves, are prone to mislead us regarding our true spiritual condition.

The moment we start to fool ourselves about our own character, we begin to compromise our influence. This is why it is so critical to take the time regularly to examine our own lives, motives, priorities, and thinking, being as honest with ourselves as we can. We often avoid such analysis because it can be painful, but ironically self-examination is part of the path to deep influence because it is in our need for His grace and ongoing transformation that we enjoy the most influence.

Here is an interesting question to ponder: Where are you

most likely to be self-deceived? It is an "ouch" question, but one that merits personal analysis. Self-deception comes in many varieties. I can be self-deceived about what motivates me in ministry or how carefully I stay within ethical boundaries. Each of us is prone to our own areas of deception that, unless understood, become spiritual traps, robbing us of influence.

On this count, a growing number of men and women have a *spiritual mentor*—a mature and insightful individual who has permission to probe their spiritual lives and ask the kinds of questions that cause them to think deeply. This is *not* about having someone tell them what to do or reveal God's will for their lives. No human can take the place of the Holy Spirit. It *is* about asking the probing questions that help discern the spiritual crevices of their lives.

People of deep influence are people of truth. They seek truth in their lives, in their relationships with God, in their relationships with people, and in their work. The pursuit of truth is a godly pursuit. Remember that the Evil One is the father of lies. As citizens living in a fallen world we are prone to believe those lies. As citizens of heaven we are committed to pursuing truth.

Truth comes to us through the Word of God and the practice of meditation on His Word, by which we measure His Word against our lives. Truth comes to us through "the Spirit of truth" (John 14:16-17), who is our counselor. And it comes to us through close, trusted friends who are given permission to speak into our lives, even when the words are hard to hear.

In the pursuit of truth and wisdom there is no substitute for a lifelong study of the Wisdom Literature in the Old Testament: Job, Psalms, Proverbs, Ecclesiastes, and Song of Songs. What passes for wisdom in our world is often foolishness to God, and vice versa. Saturating ourselves in wisdom and truth provides a filter through which we view the messages that come to us on a daily basis regarding success. The wisdom of the kingdom is foolishness to the world. The juxtaposition of a "fool" in God's eyes with the "wise" is sobering when one considers how our society defines both kinds of people.

The wisdom books challenge us to understand the fear of the Lord by following Him in all arenas of life and to examine our hearts, motives, and followership continually. They help us understand the holiness of God and His heart of truth and grace. They are a gold mine of wisdom for those who desire deep influence with others.

THE TRULY AUTHENTIC LIFE

Deep influence flows from individuals whose lives are whole. There is not a private self and a public self. Rather there is the cultivation of a life of integrity in which what you see is what you get. Through transparency with God and self, such individuals have open doors on all of their closets, no secret sins. Who they are in the dark is who they are in the light. They share a commitment to a life of integrity and honesty.

Psalm 78:72 says that David led Israel with "integrity of heart" and "skillful hands." Skillful leadership is a gift. But without a life of truth before God and man, skillful leadership is devoid of much of its power, certainly in the spiritual arena. Our leadership and influence are deeply dependent on the transparent integrity of our lives, lived with faithful consistency over the long haul.

My dream is to be known as an individual who is without guile—that is, without cunning, deception, or duplicity. There is far too much of that even in the ministry arena as agendas get in the way of authenticity, pride in the way of humility, and our vision of success in the way of what God may actually want for our lives and ministries. All too often we are seduced by our own agendas and deceive ourselves that they are God's agendas.

Such authenticity will not keep us from being misunderstood, misinterpreted, or even demonized by some from within our own circles. That is often the price of leadership. But it *will* give our lives an inherent integrity and wholeness that over time builds into deep influence. Like the practices discussed in previous chapters, that of developing transparency is a lifelong pursuit that can only be based on a correct understanding of God and ourselves, and on the discipline of regular, honest reflection. It leads, however, to deep influence.

For Reflection and Discussion

1. Are there areas where you find it hard to be appropriately transparent? What contributes to that difficulty?

2. How did the transparency of those who influenced you contribute to their influence in your life?

3. To what extent do you seek to "manage" your image rather than simply being who you are?

4. How do you remain transparent with yourself? What practices help you be honest with yourself?

5. How has your personal transparency been of benefit to you and your leadership?

CHAPTER TWELVE

GUARDING OUR HEARTS

In many ways with this chapter we come full circle. At the center of our inner lives is what the Scriptures call our *heart*. Within the heart lies the *truest* core of who we are—our relationship with God, our motives (good, bad, and sometimes mysterious even to us), that which has been brought under the lordship of Jesus, and that which makes up our shadow side. Our hearts are deeply complex and central to everything we are. Our commitment to understand and guard our hearts over the long haul of our lives is perhaps the most critical element in becoming a person of deep influence.

Life was far simpler in my younger years than it is today in my fifties, as it relates to my heart. As a young Christian I saw things as black and white, good or bad. I understood certain temptations and did my best to make choices that were pleasing to God. But I did not understand the labyrinth of my heart—its passages, rooms, closets, corners, areas where the light of Christ penetrated brilliantly and those governed by more shadow than light. Nor did I understand my ability to celebrate those areas of light and to minimize or ignore the areas of shadowy twilight.

With each passing year I understand better how much of me has yet to be transformed by Christ. I am continually amazed and often disheartened to discover another door of my heart that I have not opened to Him. With each realization I recognize how much more I need His grace today than yesterday and how important it is to understand my heart, to live in truth rather than deception (or ignorance). My spiritual pilgrimage is about understanding Him better so that I understand myself better and can bring another part of myself into alignment with Him.

People of deep influence are exegetes of their hearts. They actively seek to peel back the layers of protection that people use to avoid confronting the real self. This voluntary vulnerability allows God to transform us into what He made us to be, in every area of life—a process to be completed only when we see Him face-to-face. Deep influencers live with a profound sense of God's grace in their lives, because they are willing to acknowledge their own darkness and allow God to shine His light in dark and dangerous places within their own souls.

THE WELLSPRING OF LIFE

Solomon was one who understood the multifaceted dimensions of the heart—its capacity for good under the lordship of God and its capacity for deception and evil under the lordship of self. It was he who wrote this admonition: "Above all else, guard your heart, for everything you do flows from it" (Proverbs 4:23). His book, Ecclesiastes, is also very much a book about our hearts.

One's heart is the place from which all attitudes, motives, and actions emanate. Jesus was clear on this (see Matthew 7:15-23). Scripture is also clear on the fact that the heart of man was severely damaged by the Fall, when Adam believed Satan—that if Adam ate the fruit of the tree he would become like God (see Genesis 3:5). Interestingly, this was simply another version of Satan's ongoing effort to become like God, to usurp God (see Isaiah 14:12-14). So Satan's own competition with God became man's competition with God, with the result that "we all, like sheep, have gone astray, each of us has turned to our own way" (Isaiah 53:6), rather than God's way.

The dilemma we face is that, even though we are transformed by grace, the process of sanctification is ongoing and the ability of our hearts to deceive us is significant. This is why Christ-followers can do such damage to one another.

I think of church leaders who, in the name of "ministry," hurt others who get in their way to success. I think of Christ-followers who refuse to reconcile with another party. I think of my own ability to justify attitudes or actions that negatively impact others, in the name of furthering the gospel of Christ. It takes deep sensitivity to the Spirit of God and the Word of God—which has the ability to judge "the thoughts and attitudes of the heart" (Hebrews 4:12)—to sift through what is truly righteous in our motives, thoughts, and actions, and what is the residue of our sinful, stubborn, independent nature.

For leaders this issue is even more important because our actions impact others in a more direct way than the actions of the average person. And we have authority over others. How we use that authority is always a matter of our hearts and whether we understand the layers of our hearts, thoughts, motives, intentions, desires, and the myriad other inner influences that flow out in our actions. Like the proverbial onion, there are layers and layers of possible motivations to our actions, and getting to the real core is the constant challenge of a person of deep influence.

PEOPLE AND OUR HEARTS

Nowhere is the complexity of the leader's heart more evident than when dealing with people who cause endless grief and continually seem to be anchors that keep the ministry from moving forward. Compound that with people who spread untrue rumors and cause disruptions and who seem to have an agenda that runs counter to yours or that of the organization.

You know, I am sure, how complex such circumstances are and how easily we can take action that reflects our base instincts, rather than a pure heart. None of us, this side of heaven, will strike the perfect balance between grace and truth, but we can choose to live and act with an acute sensitivity to the motives of our heart and the direction of the Spirit.

In my younger days I spent far too much time trying to exegete others' motives and far too little time exegeting my own! Guarding my heart is all about understanding the complexity of my own heart and seeking to ensure that it reflects the wisdom of God rather than the protection of self.

How we as leaders deal with people matters. And the healthiness of the process relates directly to our degree of self-knowledge. Leadership is an ongoing journey of our growing self-understanding—that is, our understanding of what drives us, how our insecurities impact our actions, and whether we are deeply sensitive to the Spirit.

SUCCESS AND OUR HEARTS

Our motivations to succeed—whether healthy or unhealthy—have a direct impact on how we lead and how we treat the people we lead. They impact the level of drivenness that defines us and how we respond to success, if God grants it.

Success has its hidden traps. I must ask myself constantly, What is it that drives me? Is it the accolades of others telling me I have done well? Am I driven by a human definition of success or by God's definition?

It is often in success that we are vulnerable to either hurting those who get in our way or exploiting others for our purposes. After all, why should I allow others to get in the way of "God's work"? And surely the ministry I am involved in transcends the needs and concerns of others! Many of us have met people who think this way. Their ambition and drive have run over those whose paths intersected their trajectory.

One of the key indicators of our heart's condition is how we deal with success and whether it brings with it greater *pride* or greater *humility*. I both desire and fear success. I desire to have the greatest influence possible for God's purposes and the advancing of His kingdom. I fear that this very success will cause my heart to take credit for the success He granted and that I may fail the test of my heart's followership of Him.

How do we guard our hearts in seasons of success? I believe that the answer runs counter to what successful people often do. Success often makes for subtle shifts in our thinking and lives: We run faster, move away from truly authentic relationships, believe that we are better than we really are, and expect others to serve us. The way to guarding our hearts in success is exactly the opposite of these common responses.

Slow Down

Success often causes us to run faster and do more. Opportunities come to speak, to attend conferences, and to meet important people, and schedules fill till we are running on fumes. This condition is dangerous, because when we are tired and living without margin, we are at our most vulnerable. Many Christian leaders have crashed and burned in the process. Their hearts were empty, their reserves used up, and their guard down!

Here is the irony. What got us to success are usually the very practices we have studied in this book. What robs us of success is the absence of these practices, when we are running too fast and paying too little attention to what really counts. Those who are successful over the long run and who retain their deep influence are men and women who do not stray from the core—often hidden—practices we have outlined in *Deep Influence*. None of these can be done on the run. Each requires time to think, reflect, align our priorities, and stay close to God. Those who learn to say no most often are those who have tasted success and have become sought after because of that success.

Cultivate Authentic Relationships

Success breeds arrogance, unless we continue to intentionally cultivate authentic relationships with other Christ-followers who can challenge our thinking, hold us accountable, and keep us humble. Whenever I encounter arrogance, I know that these critical elements are missing and that a crash is very likely coming soon. Arrogance is the by-product of unaccountability and isolation.

Perhaps the most important people to those who have tasted success are those who knew us before we were successful in the eyes of others. They are not enamored by our new stature. They know us for who we really are, and our relationships are not based on fame or accolades. Like God, they are not enamored by the new persona but look for the authentic heart in us.

Pay Close Attention to Your Shadow Side

If anyone needs to understand and be aware of his or her shadow side, it is the one who has tasted success. In success we are tempted to believe that we are better than we really are—to minimize our weaknesses and exaggerate our strengths. The Evil One is constantly looking for opportunities to trip us up, and when we distort our self-concept, we become prime meat for him.

One of the keys to guarding our hearts is paying more attention to our shadow side as we experience success. This practice reminds us of our spiritual frailty, of our need for God's grace on a daily basis, and that we are merely cracked pots whom God uses in His redemption plan for our world. Our shadow side—that part of us that still needs to be sanctified by Christ—is a daily reminder that we are no different from any of God's other children. It humbles us and causes us to fall before the cross daily for grace and forgiveness.

Intentionally Serve Others

One of the deadly results of success is the temptation to think that others should be serving us rather than we, them. As the leader of a large organization I am acutely aware of privileges that I enjoy. I have greater autonomy over my priorities and schedule, authority to make decisions that impact others, and the ability to build a team that covers for my weaknesses and allows me to live in my sweet spot most of the time. I also receive recognition that others may not normally receive. These are privileges of position. There are also temptations to believe that I am *special* and *entitled*.

Nothing could be farther from the truth! The posture of Jesus and His disciples is the posture of a servant who came to serve. A servant's attitude guards our hearts and keeps us grounded in the Christian call to serve others as Christ served and serves us. It helps us resist the insidious move toward pride and privilege and helps us remember the source of our success—the gracious hand of God and those who make up our teams and organizations.

DISCOURAGEMENT AND OUR HEARTS

Ironically, we must guard our hearts during times of failure and discouragement, as well as times of success. Success may cause us to take our eyes off of our Lord and focus on ourselves; failure and discouragement have the potential to do the same thing.

My own story related in these pages illustrates how dangerous failure and discouragement can be. I came very close to walking away from full-time ministry altogether. I know both vocational and avocational ministry-driven individuals who have done that in the face of great difficulties. I am sobered by the implications for my own life and ministry impact had I chosen to walk away from the call of God.

Times of failure—real or perceived—and of disillusionment are critical for the health of our hearts, as they force us to choose where we will put our trust in the face of impossible circumstances. We are forced into the decision to put our faith in our heavenly Father—just as were those listed in Hebrews 11—even when we cannot see a way out.

Failure and discouragement force a life-changing choice. Will I continue to trust and follow closely after Christ, or will I settle for a diminished and wounded life? Failure is never final unless *we* allow it to be. We make the choice as to whether we will move on and follow Him in the midst of our pain or allow our pain to pull us away from Him. It is always *our* choice and *our* move.

One of the common responses to discouragement and failure is cynicism. All of us have reason to be cynical about people—especially those who claim to be Christ-followers and do things unworthy of His name. Yet cynicism is a destructive attitude and hurts our hearts. It causes us to doubt the good intentions of others, robs us of our ability to trust, and skews our attitude toward others. Think about this: What if God chose to be cynical toward us? Our actions and attitudes often deserve it, yet He chooses to love and believe the best in us. Cynicism robs us of the ability to love and believe the best.

In my fifties, I am deeply realistic about the realities of people and situations I face. What keeps me from cynicism is my awareness of my own struggles, failures, and imperfections, as well as a deep but imperfect desire for righteousness. I am thankful that God is not cynical with me, and I want to resist the temptation to be cynical toward others. Paul meant it when he wrote his letters to the "saints," even when he needed to chastise and take people to task as he did in 1 and 2 Corinthians. We are saints—holy ones—even in our imperfections and struggles, and we want to treat all of God's people in that light—even those who irritate us.

HEARTS THAT GO THE DISTANCE

Our natural inclination in the middle and later years is to allow ourselves to revert to autopilot, paying *less* rather than *more* attention to those aspects of our inner lives that truly matter. This is living in the danger zone, because when we ignore the hidden practices we have explored in this book, our influence wanes. It is those who press in more diligently during these years who end well and develop the deepest influence. Their spiritual lives are enriched by a life of experience, a deeper understanding of themselves, and a closer followership of their Lord. They intentionally choose to go the distance.

Perhaps one of the most significant measures we can take in the second half of life is to slow down so that we have time to think, reflect, analyze, meditate, and deeply consider our inner lives. Our commitment to the hidden practices is the key to our deepest influence and most lasting legacy, but these practices cannot be microwaved on the run. They take time and require deep reflection.

The pace at which we run can be an excuse to ignore what we don't want to face, but what we know is most important. When I am quiet, without distractions, I am often reminded of unfinished business, of pockets of my heart that need attention, of sinful ways of which I don't like to be reminded. Yet until I face these issues honestly, I cannot deal with them. When I look deeply, I don't always like what I see in my own heart, but that is where renovation can start!

My father, to whom this book is dedicated, passed away in 2012 at age eighty-five. His accomplishments were many, if one considers degrees and résumés: civil engineer, theologian, church planter, missionary, doctor, surgeon, author, well-known adult Sunday school teacher. All of those accomplishments fade, however, when compared to the quiet and deep influence he has had with thousands of people along the journey, from all parts of the world. His legacy is found in people who through his influence discovered a lasting relationship with Christ. We see it in those who chose to follow more closely after God—some at great sacrifice—because of his deep influence on their lives.

One of the things I appreciate about Dad is that he never quit growing. He was passionate about Scripture and about knowing and serving God. For years we would compete as to how many books we read. He loved to talk about theology, and we engaged in robust discussions, not always seeing eye to eye. In his later years he wrote a book called *Discovering the Bible*, which he self-published until a major publisher picked it up. Many have used this tool as they read through Scripture.

Where are the wise men and women of our generation who provide models and who influence others toward eternal values? Where are those men and women who invest their lives in the next generation rather than in their own self-ish fulfillment? Where are those who don't hang it all up at retirement but continue to stay engaged in ministry till the end? Where are those who understand that we have all of eternity to enjoy one another and Christ, but just a few years to influence others on this side of eternity?

Each day of our lives we make an investment of some kind. What investment are you making today? Are you investing in those hidden practices that will result in a legacy of deep influence, or have you settled for something shallow and merely temporal? My guess is that if you are reading this book, you are committed to becoming a person of the deep-est influence you can be.

If you are a young leader, I would challenge you to a life-time of cultivating the hidden practices that make for deep influence. You will never regret paying attention to these practices, but you will one day regret *not* doing so if you push them aside. If you are in your middle or later years, I encourage you to finish well and go the distance, continuing to learn, grow, and allow God's heart to transform yours. Thereby you will be that person of deep influence to others.

And may He give you joy in the journey.

For Reflection and Discussion

1. How do you manage the issues of your heart, knowing that who you are, what you do, and how you lead all spring out of the content of your heart?

2. How do you guard your heart in success? How do you guard it in times of discouragement and failure?

3. What is your strategy for ensuring that your motives are right in dealing with people who irritate you?

4. Identify three significant takeaways from this book. What is your first step for each one?

Notes

CHAPTER 3: SUFFERING AND LEADERSHIP

1. A. W. Tozer, *The Root of the Righteous* (Harrisburg: Christian Publications Inc., 1955), 137.

CHAPTER 7: LEADING FROM WHO GOD MADE *ME* TO BE

1. T. J. Addington, *Leading from the Sandbox* (Colorado Springs: NavPress, 2010), 17.

CHAPTER 9: THINKING LIKE A CONTRARIAN

1. John Bessant, Kathrin Möslein, and Bettina von Stamm, "In Search of Innovation," *The Wall Street Journal*, June 22, 2009, http://online.wsj.com /news/articles/SB20001424052970204830304574133562888635626.
2. Rick Warren, *The Purpose-Driven Church* (Grand Rapids: Zondervan, 1995), 144-145.
3. Henri Nouwen, *The Essential Henri Nouwen*, ed. Robert A. Jonas (Boston: Shambhala, 2009), 100.

About the Author

T. J. Addington is a Senior Vice President with the EFCA and the leader of ReachGlobal, the international mission of the EFCA. He has served as a pastor, consultant, and denominational leader.

Over the past twenty-five years, T. J. has consulted with numerous churches and Christian non-profit organizations in the areas of healthy leaders, intentional leadership, governance systems, and dealing with issues of organizational health and strategy. In addition he has been a leadership mentor and trainer to many. He resides with his wife of 38 years, Mary Ann, in Oakdale, MN, and is the father of two sons and has two grandsons.

T. J. is the author of five books: *High-Impact Church Boards*; *Leading from the Sandbox*; *Live Like You Mean It*; *When Life Comes Undone*; and *Deep Influence*. In his spare time T. J. is an avid fly fisherman and a lover of books, traveling, and writing.

We are all fellow pilgrims on a journey toward better followership of Jesus and leadership of people. If you would like to share something of your journey with T. J., you can contact him at tjaddington@gmail.com.